Better Homes and Gardens®

POULTRY

© Copyright 1986 by Meredith Corporation, Des Moines, Iowa.
All Rights Reserved. Printed in the United States of America.
First Edition. First Printing.
Library of Congress Catalog Card Number: 85-61420
ISBN: 0-696-02194-3

BETTER HOMES AND GARDENS® BOOKS

Editor Gerald M. Knox
Art Director Ernest Shelton
Managing Editor David A. Kirchner
Copy and Production Editors James D. Blume, Marsha Jahns, Mary Helen Schiltz, Carl Voss

Food and Nutrition Editor Nancy Byal
Department Head—Cook Books Sharyl Heiken
Associate Department Heads Sandra Granseth, Rosemary C. Hutchinson, Elizabeth Woolever
Senior Food Editors Julia Malloy, Marcia Stanley, Joyce Trollope
Associate Food Editors Barbara Atkins, Linda Foley, Linda Henry, Lynn Hoppe,
Jill Johnson, Mary Jo Plutt, Maureen Powers, Martha Schiel
Recipe Development Editor Marion Viall
Test Kitchen Director Sharon Stilwell
Test Kitchen Photo Studio Director Janet Pittman
Test Kitchen Home Economists Jean Brekke, Kay Cargill, Marilyn Cornelius, Jennifer Darling,
Maryellyn Krantz, Lynelle Munn, Dianna Nolin, Marge Steenson,
Cynthia Volcko

Associate Art Directors Linda Ford Vermie, Neoma Alt West, Randall Yontz
Assistant Art Directors Lynda Haupert, Harijs Priekulis, Tom Wegner
Senior Graphic Designers Mike Eagleton, Stan Sams, Darla Whipple-Frain
Graphic Designers Mike Burns, Sally Cooper, Jack Murphy,
Brian D. Wignall, Kimberly Zarley

Vice President, Editorial Director Doris Eby
Executive Director, Editorial Services Duane L. Gregg

Senior Vice President, General Manager Fred Stines
Director of Publishing Robert B. Nelson
Vice President, Retail Marketing Jamie Martin
Vice President, Direct Marketing Arthur Heydendael

Poultry
Editor Barbara Atkins
Copy and Production Editor Mary Helen Schiltz
Graphic Designer Lynda Haupert
Electronic Text Processor Donna Russell
Photographers Michael Jensen and Sean Fitzgerald
Food Stylists Suzanne Finley, Dianna Nolin, Janet Pittman, Maria Rolandelli
Contributing Illustrator Thomas Rosborough

On the cover
Wild-Rice-Stuffed Turkey (see recipe, page 16).

Our seal assures you that every recipe in *Poultry* has been tested in the Better Homes and Gardens® Test Kitchen. This means that each recipe is practical and reliable, and meets our high standards of taste appeal.

What characteristics would you wish for in a "perfect" food? Perhaps tasty, appealing, nutritious, economical, and versatile? Then poultry just may be a wish come true. It boasts each of these virtues!

Poultry's well-rounded flavor appeals to a wide range of tastes. And it's a wholesome source of low-fat protein, as well as a good food bargain.

Versatility is poultry's middle name. It can be as luxurious as Chicken Cordon Bleu or as humble as the time-honored Chicken and Dumplings.

And as for ways to cook it . . . well, imagination is the only limit. Roast, barbecue, pan-fry, fricassee, or stew. *You* choose the method that best fits *your* needs.

From the tasteful simplicity of a roasted bird to the sheer elegance of a stuffed boneless chicken, *Poultry* offers something for everyone.

Contents

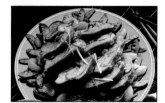

Golden Roasted Poultry

Looking for a new twist on a good ol' roast chicken dinner? Then you've come to the right place! This chapter is filled with delightfully new, easy-to-fix, and tasty-to-eat roast poultry recipes.

You'll find everything from the ever-popular and humble chicken to the classy, special-occasion squab—all simply rubbed or brushed with flavorful ingredients.

And if this is your first cooking adventure with poultry . . . relax. All you'll need to know to begin is in a handy Shopper's Guide.

Roast Herbed Chicken

Roast Herbed Chicken

So easy to make . . . so pretty to serve.

1 **2½-to 3-pound broiler-fryer chicken**
  Cooking oil *or* melted butter
1 **teaspoon dried basil**
1 **teaspoon dried oregano**
1 **teaspoon dried parsley flakes**
½ **teaspoon onion salt**
½ **teaspoon dried marjoram**
  Apple wedges (optional)
  Celery leaves (optional)

Rinse bird, then pat dry (see photo 1). Brush bird with oil or butter. In a small mixing bowl combine basil, oregano, parsley, onion salt, and marjoram; crush slightly. Rub onto bird (see photo 2). Tie legs together; pull neck skin to back and twist wing tips under (see photo 3).

Place bird, breast side up, on a rack in a shallow roasting pan. Roast, uncovered, in a 375° oven 1¼ to 1½ hours or till done (see photo 4). Spoon drippings over bird occasionally.

Cover, then let stand 15 minutes before carving (see page 19). If desired, garnish with apple wedges and celery leaves. Makes 6 servings.

Roast Herbed Quail: Prepare Roast Herbed Chicken as above, *except* substitute eight 4- to 6-ounce plucked *quail* for chicken. Tie legs of each quail together. Omit pulling neck skin to back. Twist wing tips under (see photo 3). Place on a rack in a shallow roasting pan; cover loosely with foil. Roast in a 375° oven 40 to 50 minutes or till done (see photo 4). Serve quail whole. Makes 4 servings.

1 Remove the giblets. Rinse the bird inside and out under cold running water, as shown. Let any excess water run off. Pat dry with paper towels.

3 Tie the legs together with string. If the tail is present, tie the legs to it. Then pull the neck skin to the back of the bird. Twist the wing tips under the back so they hold the neck skin in place.

2 Use your fingers to rub the herb mixture onto the bird's skin and inside the body cavity.

4 To test for doneness, grasp the end of the drumstick with a paper towel. It should move up and down and twist easily in the socket.

Or, pierce the thigh meat with a fork. The meat should feel tender and the juices should be clear, not pink.

A meat thermometer inserted into the thigh should register 180° to 185°. In a turkey breast half, the thermometer should register 170°.

Garlic Roast Chicken

1 **2½- to 3-pound broiler-fryer chicken**
1 **tablespoon olive oil *or* cooking oil**
1 **to 1¼ teaspoons garlic powder**

Rinse bird, then pat dry (see photo 1, page 9). Season cavity with salt. Combine oil and garlic powder. Rub onto bird (see photo 2, page 9). Tie legs together; pull neck skin to back and twist wing tips under (see photo 3, page 9).

Place bird, breast side up, on a rack in a shallow roasting pan. Roast, uncovered, in a 375° oven 1¼ to 1½ hours or till done (see photo 4, page 9). Spoon drippings over bird occasionally.

Cover, then let stand 15 minutes before carving (see page 19). Makes 6 servings.

Thawing Frozen Poultry

Observing traffic laws makes driving a whole lot safer. Likewise, following proper instructions for thawing frozen poultry makes a cooked bird safer to eat, too. Here are the "rules of the road."

Place poultry, in its original wrapping, on a tray in the refrigerator. Allow 24 hours of thawing time for every 5 pounds.

For fast thawing, place poultry, in its original wrapping, in a sink or large bowl. Cover with *cold* water; change water often. Allow ½ hour thawing time per pound.

Never let poultry stand at room temperature to thaw. The bacteria that cause food poisoning grow at these temperatures.

Four-Spice Turkey Breast

Skewering the skin to the bottom edge of the meat prevents it from shrinking during roasting.

1 **2½- to 3½-pound turkey breast half with bone**
2 **tablespoons cooking oil**
½ **teaspoon ground allspice**
½ **teaspoon ground cinnamon**
½ **teaspoon ground nutmeg**
¼ **teaspoon ground ginger**

Rinse turkey, then pat dry (see photo 1, page 9). In a small mixing bowl combine oil, allspice, cinnamon, nutmeg, and ginger. Rub spice mixture onto turkey (see photo 2, page 9). Insert small skewers or wooden toothpicks to hold the skin and meat together along the bottom edge of breast half.

Place, skin side up, on a rack in a shallow roasting pan. Insert a meat thermometer into center of breast. Cover turkey loosely with foil. Roast in a 325° oven 2½ to 3 hours or till the thermometer registers 170° (see photo 4, page 9). Uncover the last 30 minutes. Spoon drippings over turkey occasionally.

Cover, then let stand 15 minutes before carving. To carve, start at outside of breast half and slice downward, keeping slices thin and even. Start each new slice slightly higher up on the breast. Makes 6 servings.

Four-Spice Chicken: Prepare Four-Spice Turkey Breast as above, *except* substitute one 2½- to 3-pound *broiler-fryer chicken* for turkey. Roast, uncovered, in a 375° oven 1¼ to 1½ hours or till done (see photo 4, page 9). Spoon drippings over bird occasionally. Cover, then let stand 15 minutes before carving (see page 19). Makes 6 servings.

Shopper's Guide

Types of Poultry

Broiler-fryer chickens are young birds that are about 7 weeks old and weigh 2 to 5 pounds. The average is about 3 pounds. Allow about ½ pound for each serving.

Roasting chickens are usually about 10 weeks old and weigh over 5 pounds. Allow about ½ pound for each serving.

Capons are neutered male chickens. They have a fat layer under the skin that ensures tender meat even though the birds are larger. Capons are about 16 weeks old and weigh 5 to 9 pounds. Allow about ½ pound for each serving.

Cornish game hens are special hybrid birds, about 4 to 5 weeks old and weighing 1 to 1½ pounds. Allow ½ bird per serving.

Turkeys are under 8 months old and weigh anywhere from 6 to 24 pounds. Allow ¾ to 1 pound for each serving.

Domestic ducklings are 7 to 8 weeks old, weigh 3 to 5 pounds, and usually are sold frozen. Allow 1 pound for each serving. Birds labeled duck are older and heavier.

Domestic geese are 4 to 6 months old. They weigh from 6 to 14 pounds (8 to 10 pounds is the most common purchased weight). Allow 1 pound for each serving.

Domestic quail are tiny birds and weigh 4 to 6 ounces. Allow 2 birds per serving.

Domestic pheasant vary in size from 2 to 3 pounds, depending on the age and time of year. Two 2-pound pheasant, typically found early in the growing season, may be substituted for one 3-pound bird. Pheasant are leaner than chicken. Allow about ½ pound for each serving.

Squabs are 4-week-old domesticated pigeons. They weigh between 12 and 14 ounces and are primarily dark meat. Allow 1 bird for each serving.

Buying and Storing Poultry

Look for plump, meaty birds. The skin should be clean, smooth, and free of discoloration. A USDA Grade A mark assures these characteristics. Make sure the package is not broken and there are no unusual odors.

You can store uncooked poultry in its supermarket wrapping in the refrigerator (40°F) for up to 2 days. For longer storage, wrap the supermarket package in foil, freezer paper, or a plastic freezer bag and store in the freezer. Chicken pieces keep 9 months; turkey pieces, 6 months. Whole chickens and turkeys keep 12 months, and whole ducks and geese keep 6 months. Wrap the giblets separately; store in the freezer 3 to 4 months. Freeze cooked poultry dishes 4 to 6 months. *Do not thaw, then refreeze, uncooked or cooked poultry.* Doing so decreases the quality and flavor.

Game Birds

We used *domestic* birds in recipe testing and recommend you use them as well. Since domestic birds are raised on game farms and receive feed, they are fattier than their wild counterparts. Thus, the timings and cooking methods for the two types of birds differ considerably. For example, *domestic* geese and ducklings must have their skin pricked before roasting to let the fat escape. However, *wild* geese and ducklings need to be larded (rubbed with oil or butter) to ensure moistness.

There are several ways to obtain domestic game. Many supermarkets stock it in the freezer section. Some mail order catalogs sell game birds. Check the yellow pages for game farm listings. Or ask local restaurateurs who serve game for sources.

Dill-Buttered Cornish Hens

Here's a "dill-icious" butter rub that will leave taste buds longing for just one more bite.

2 1- to 1½-pound Cornish game hens
2 tablespoons butter *or* margarine, softened
1 tablespoon snipped fresh dill *or* 1 teaspoon dried dillweed

Rinse hens, then pat dry (see photo 1, page 9). Season cavities with salt. In a small mixing bowl combine butter and dill. Rub *half* of the mixture onto *each* hen (see photo 2, page 9). Tie legs together; pull neck skin to back and twist wing tips under (see photo 3, page 9).

Place birds, breast side up, on a rack in a shallow roasting pan. Cover loosely with foil. Roast in a 375° oven for 30 minutes. Uncover hens. Roast 45 to 55 minutes more or till done (see photo 4, page 9). Baste occasionally with drippings. To serve, halve hens lengthwise. Makes 4 servings.

Dill-Buttered Chicken: Prepare Dill-Buttered Cornish Hens as above, *except* substitute one 2½- to 3-pound *broiler-fryer chicken* for hens. Rub with entire butter mixture (see photo 2, page 9). Do not cover. Roast in a 375° oven 1¼ to 1½ hours or till done (see photo 4, page 9). Cover, then let stand 15 minutes before carving (see page 19). Makes 6 servings.

Honey-Mustard Squabs

A golden glaze that's delicately flavored with the natural sweetness of honey.

4 12- to 14-ounce squabs
2 tablespoons butter *or* margarine, melted
2 tablespoons honey
1 teaspoon prepared mustard
Lemon leaves (optional)
Lemon slices (optional)

Rinse birds, then pat dry (see photo 1, page 9). Rub cavities with salt. Tie legs together; if present, pull neck skin to back and twist wing tips under (see photo 3, page 9).

Place birds, breast side up, on a rack in a shallow roasting pan. Cover loosely with foil. Roast in a 375° oven for 30 minutes.

Meanwhile, in a small mixing bowl combine butter or margarine, honey, and mustard. Uncover birds; brush with some of the butter mixture. Roast, uncovered, 30 to 40 minutes more or till done (see photo 4, page 9). Brush occasionally with butter mixture. Serve squabs whole. If desired, garnish with lemon leaves and lemon slices. Makes 4 servings.

Honey-Mustard Hens: Prepare the Honey-Mustard Squabs as above, *except* substitute two 1- to 1½-pound *Cornish game hens* for squabs. Cover loosely with foil. Roast in a 375° oven 30 minutes. Uncover birds; brush with some of the butter mixture. Roast, uncovered, 45 to 55 minutes more or till done (see photo 4, page 9). Brush occasionally with butter mixture. To serve, halve hens lengthwise. Makes 4 servings.

▶ *Pictured opposite:*
Honey-Mustard Squabs

Stuffed And Roasted Birds

When family and friends gather together, you'll likely want to treat them to a special celebration. Why not serve one of the mouth-watering stuffed birds from the tempting selection offered here?

Pick the recipe that best fits the size of your gathering. Then follow our easy instructions for smashing results. Your home-cooked feast is sure to help celebrate the joy of the occasion.

Wild-Rice-Stuffed Turkey

Wild-Rice-Stuffed Turkey

2	6-ounce packages long grain and wild rice mix
½	pound Canadian-style bacon, diced
½	cup sliced green onion
2	cloves garlic, minced
¼	cup butter *or* margarine
1	8-ounce can water chestnuts, drained and chopped
1	14- to 16-pound turkey
	Cooking oil *or* melted butter

For stuffing, prepare rice mix according to package directions. In a 12-inch skillet cook and stir bacon, onion, and garlic in hot butter or margarine about 5 minutes or till onion is tender. Stir in ¼ cup *water* and ¼ teaspoon *pepper*. In a large mixing bowl combine rice, onion mixture, and water chestnuts. Toss till well mixed.

Rinse bird, then pat dry. Season body cavity with salt. Spoon stuffing into neck cavity (see photo 1). Skewer neck skin to back (see photo 2). Spoon stuffing into body cavity. Tuck drumsticks under tail skin (see photo 3). Twist wing tips under (see photo 3, page 9).

Place bird, breast side up, on a rack in a shallow roasting pan. Brush with oil or butter. Insert a meat thermometer (see photo 4). Cover bird loosely with foil. Place any remaining stuffing in a casserole; cover and chill. Roast turkey in a 325° oven 4½ to 5 hours or till thermometer registers 180° to 185° (see photo 4, page 9). Cut band of skin between legs after 3½ hours. Uncover bird and add stuffing in covered casserole to the oven the last 45 minutes of roasting.

Cover bird; let stand 20 minutes before carving (see page 19). Garnish with spiced crab apples and celery leaves, if desired. Serves 20 to 22.

Wild-Rice-Stuffed Chicken: Prepare Wild-Rice-Stuffed Turkey as above, *except* substitute one 2½- to 3-pound *broiler-fryer chicken* for turkey and halve remaining ingredients. Roast, uncovered, in a 375° oven 1¼ to 1½ hours or till done (see photo 4, page 9). Serves 6.

1 To stuff the bird, begin by lightly spooning some of the stuffing into the neck cavity. Spoon the stuffing in loosely; *do not pack it.* This leaves room for the stuffing to expand during roasting. Use these same techniques for stuffing the body cavity.

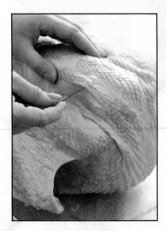

2 Pull the neck skin over the stuffing to the back of the bird. Fasten the neck skin securely to the back with a small wooden or metal skewer.

3 If the bird has a band of skin across the tail, tuck the ends of the drumsticks under the band, as shown. If the band of skin is not present, tie the legs securely to the tail with string. Securing the legs and tail in this manner maintains an attractive shape during roasting.

4 Insert a meat thermometer in the center of the inside thigh muscle, making sure the bulb of the thermometer does not touch the bone. If the bulb touches the bone, the thermometer will give an inaccurate reading. The bird is done when the thermometer registers 180° to 185°.

Raisin-Sausage-Stuffed Cornish Hens

Our food editors rated the flavor of this fluffy, fruit stuffing outstanding.

2 **1- to 1½-pound Cornish game hens**
  Cooking oil *or* melted butter
1 **tablespoon orange juice**
1½ **teaspoons butter *or* margarine, melted**
¼ **pound bulk pork sausage**
⅓ **cup chopped celery**
1½ **cups soft bread crumbs (2 slices)**
½ **cup light raisins**
⅓ **cup chopped walnuts**
¼ **teaspoon ground ginger**
¼ **teaspoon ground nutmeg**
¼ **teaspoon finely shredded orange peel**
  Dash pepper
⅓ **cup orange juice**
2 **tablespoons butter *or* margarine, melted**

Rinse hens; pat dry. Season body cavities with salt. Skewer neck skin to back (see photo 2, page 16). Tie legs to tail (see photo 3, page 17). Twist wing tips under (see photo 3, page 9).

Place birds, breast side up, on a rack in a shallow roasting pan. Brush with oil or butter. Cover loosely with foil. Roast in a 375° oven 30 minutes. Combine 1 tablespoon juice and 1½ teaspoons butter or margarine. Uncover birds; brush with juice mixture. Roast 45 to 55 minutes more or till done (see photo 4, page 9).

Meanwhile, in a 10-inch skillet cook sausage and celery till meat is brown; drain. In a large mixing bowl combine sausage, celery, bread, raisins, nuts, ginger, nutmeg, orange peel, and pepper. Drizzle with ⅓ cup orange juice and 2 tablespoons butter or margarine. Toss lightly till well mixed. Place stuffing in a 1-quart casserole; cover and chill. Add covered casserole to the oven the last 20 to 30 minutes of roasting.

To serve, halve hens lengthwise. Place stuffing in 4 mounds on a warm platter; top each mound with a hen half. Garnish with parsley sprigs, if desired. Makes 4 servings.

Bourbon-Sauced Pheasant

A spicy stuffing with a pretty, "plum good" glaze.

1 **cup chopped mixed dried fruit**
1 **5½-ounce can apricot nectar**
⅓ **cup bourbon**
3½ **cups bread cubes (about 5 slices)**
½ **cup chopped pecans**
½ **teaspoon ground cinnamon**
3 **tablespoons butter *or* margarine, melted**
1 **3-pound domestic pheasant**
2 **slices bacon, halved crosswise**
¼ **cup plum jelly**

In a small saucepan combine dried fruit, nectar, and bourbon. Bring to boiling. Reduce heat, then cover and simmer for 5 minutes. Remove from heat. Let stand for 15 minutes. Drain, reserving liquid.

Meanwhile, place bread cubes in a large shallow baking pan. Toast in a 375° oven 10 to 15 minutes or till dried. In a large mixing bowl combine bread, nuts, and cinnamon. Drizzle with butter or margarine and ¼ *cup* reserved liquid. Toss lightly till well mixed. Stir in fruit.

Rinse bird; pat dry. Season body cavity with salt. Skewer neck skin to back (see photo 2, page 16). Spoon stuffing into body cavity (see photo 1, page 16). Tie legs to tail (see photo 3, page 17). Twist wing tips under (see photo 3, page 9).

Place bird, breast side up, on a rack in a shallow roasting pan. Lay bacon over breast. Roast in a 350° oven 1½ to 1¾ hours or till done (see photo 4, page 9). Measure remaining stuffing. For *each* cup, stir in 1 tablespoon *water*. Place in a casserole; cover and chill. Add covered casserole to oven the last 30 minutes of roasting.

In a small saucepan heat and stir jelly with remaining reserved liquid (about 1 tablespoon) till jelly melts. Discard bacon; baste pheasant frequently with plum sauce the last 15 minutes.

Cover bird; let stand for 15 minutes before carving (see page 19). Makes 6 servings.

Carving a Roasted Bird

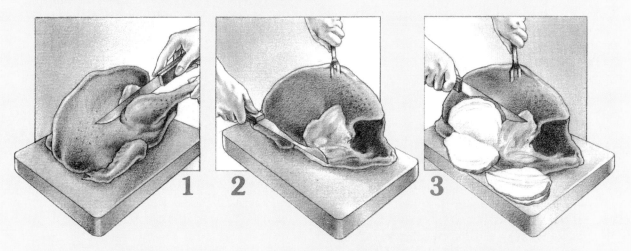

Do you avoid carving that spectacular roasted bird because it might look more butchered than carved? Relax. Although graceful carving can be considered an art, it is one you can easily learn.

Begin with a sharp carving knife (or an electric knife for ease and speed). Then simply follow our step-by-step directions and illustrations. Next time you'll find yourself carving with the ease of a pro.

After removing the bird from the oven, let it stand for 15 to 20 minutes before carving. Cover it with foil to keep it warm. Standing lets the flesh firm up so the carved slices will hold together.

Place the bird on a carving board. If the bird is stuffed, remove the stuffing. Then, grasp the tip of one drumstick with your fingers and pull the leg away from the body. Cut through the skin and meat between the drumstick-thigh piece and body (see illustration 1). This exposes the joint where the thighbone and backbone connect. With the tip of the knife, disjoint the thighbone from the backbone by cutting through the joint. Repeat on the other side.

To separate the thigh and drumstick, cut through the joint where the leg and thigh bones meet. Repeat on the other piece.

Hold the drumstick vertically by the tip with the large end down. Slice the meat parallel to the bone and under some tendons, turning the leg to get even slices. Next, slice the thigh meat by cutting slices parallel to the bone. Repeat with the remaining drumstick and thigh. This step applies only to larger birds. The legs and thighs of smaller birds are usually served whole.

Before carving the breast meat, make a deep horizontal cut into the breast above each wing (see illustration 2). This cut will be the end point of the breast meat slices.

Beginning at the outer edge of one side of the breast, cut slices from the top of the breast down to the horizontal cut (see illustration 3). Make the slices thin and even. Final smaller slices can follow the curve of the breastbone. Repeat on other side of breast.

Remove wings by cutting through the joint where the wing bone and backbone meet.

Perfectly Poached Poultry

Health-conscious? Here's a really easy way to make light-to-eat poultry—cook it in a simmering liquid.

Since you don't use oil, there aren't any added calories from fat. But the dishes are still chock-full of flavor and color.

The secret? We chose cooking liquids, seasonings, and garnishes that will delight both the taste buds and the eyes. Our hunch is no one will guess just how healthy and sensible these dishes are!

Sweet 'n' Sour Turkey

Sweet 'n' Sour Turkey

1 2-pound turkey thigh
1 6-ounce can frozen pineapple juice
   concentrate, thawed
½ cup red wine vinegar
3 tablespoons soy sauce
¼ teaspoon garlic powder
¼ teaspoon ground ginger
2 6-ounce packages frozen pea pods
1 11-ounce can mandarin orange sections,
   drained

Rinse poultry. In a 10-inch skillet combine juice concentrate, vinegar, soy, garlic powder, and ginger. Bring to boiling. Carefully add turkey (see photo 1). Reduce heat; cover and simmer 1¼ hours or till tender (see photo 5, page 35).

Use a slotted spoon and fork to transfer turkey to a carving board. Remove the thighbone (see photo 2). Slice the meat. Cover and keep warm.

For sauce, skim fat from pan juices (see photo 3). Bring juices to boiling. Boil, uncovered, stirring occasionally, 7 to 8 minutes or till juices are reduced to ¾ cup (see photo 4).

Meanwhile, cook pea pods according to package directions; drain. Toss with orange sections. Transfer to a serving platter; arrange sliced turkey on top. Pour sauce over turkey. If desired, garnish with green onion strips. Serves 4.

1 Use a long spatula, slotted spoon, or tongs to carefully lower the turkey thigh into the boiling liquid in the skillet. Be careful not to drop the turkey into the skillet as this may dangerously splatter the boiling liquid.

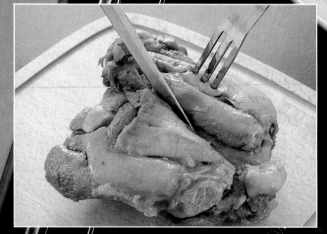

2 Transfer the turkey thigh from the cooking liquid to a carving board. With the thigh bone side up, make a cut along the bone in order to free the meat from the bone, as shown. Pull or scrape the remainder of the meat away from the bone. Remove and discard the thighbone.

3 Use a metal spoon to skim off the fat that rises to the surface of the pan juices.

4 Boil the juices, uncovered, till they are reduced to ¾ cup. Stir occasionally.

To judge when the juices have been reduced enough, pour them into a measuring cup. If there is more than ¾ cup, return them to the pan and continue boiling. Repeat the procedure until there is only ¾ cup.

Cranberry-Sauced Turkey Steaks

Convenient turkey steaks let you create Thanksgiving flavors in just 30 minutes.

4   **turkey breast tenderloin steaks (1 pound total)**
1   **cup water**
⅓   **cup dry white wine**
2   **small onions, cut into thin wedges**
2   **bay leaves**
1   **medium carrot, thinly bias sliced**
1   **stalk celery, thinly bias sliced**
1   **8-ounce can whole cranberry sauce**
1   **tablespoon dry white wine**

Rinse poultry. In a 12-inch skillet combine water, ⅓ cup wine, onions, and bay leaves. Bring to boiling. Reduce heat; cover and simmer 5 minutes. Carefully add turkey, carrot, and celery (see photo 1, page 22). Cover; simmer 20 minutes more or till tender (see photo 5, page 35).

In a small saucepan stir cranberry sauce over low heat till heated through. Add 1 tablespoon wine. Drain turkey and vegetables; transfer to a serving platter. Spoon cranberry sauce mixture over turkey and vegetables. Makes 4 servings.

Chicken in Herbed Tomato Sauce

Ladle this generously sauced chicken over spaghetti or linguine for a scrumptious Italian dinner.

1½ **pounds meaty chicken pieces (breast, thighs, drumsticks)**
1   **8-ounce can tomato sauce**
½   **cup tomato juice**
1   **medium onion, chopped (½ cup)**
1   **teaspoon dried basil, crushed**
1   **teaspoon dried oregano, crushed**
½   **teaspoon dried rosemary, crushed**
¼   **teaspoon dried thyme, crushed**

Rinse poultry. In a 10-inch skillet combine tomato sauce, juice, onion, basil, oregano, rosemary, and thyme. Bring to boiling. Carefully add chicken (see photo 1, page 22). Reduce heat, then cover and simmer for 20 to 25 minutes or till tender (see photo 5, page 35). Use a slotted spoon to transfer chicken to a serving platter. Cover and keep warm.

For sauce, skim fat from tomato mixture (see photo 3, page 23). Bring tomato mixture to boiling. Reduce heat, then simmer, stirring occasionally, 8 minutes or till sauce is reduced to 1 cup (see photo 4, page 23). Spoon sauce over chicken. Makes 4 servings.

Poaching Chicken

Often you need plain cooked chicken for chicken salads (see pages 26 to 31) or your favorite chicken casserole (see pages 56 to 63). If leftover roasted chicken isn't handy, poached chicken is an easy substitute.

Start with 2 whole medium chicken breasts (1½ pounds total), halved lengthwise. *Or,* use ¾ pound purchased boneless chicken breasts. Either yields about 2 cups cut-up cooked chicken.

In a 10-inch skillet bring 1⅓ cups water to boiling. Carefully add chicken. Reduce heat. Cover and simmer 20 to 25 minutes or till tender. Drain. Cool chicken; cut up.

Microwaving is another fast way to cook chicken (see tip box, page 60). Place breasts in a 1½-quart nonmetal casserole. *Do not add liquid.* Micro-cook, covered, on 100% power (HIGH) 5 to 6 minutes or till tender. Turn breasts over after 2½ minutes.

Curry- and Wine-Sauced Chicken

For a pretty color contrast, serve the chicken on a bed of steamed asparagus spears.

2 whole medium chicken breasts
    (1½ pounds total), halved lengthwise
½ cup dry white wine
1 2½-ounce jar sliced mushrooms
2 cloves garlic, minced
1½ to 2 teaspoons curry powder
¼ teaspoon ground red pepper
    Steamed asparagus spears (optional)

Rinse poultry. In a 10-inch skillet combine wine, *undrained* mushrooms, garlic, curry powder, and pepper. Bring to boiling. Carefully add chicken (see photo 1, page 22). Reduce heat, then cover and simmer for 20 to 25 minutes or till tender (see photo 5, page 35). Use a slotted spoon to transfer chicken to a serving platter. Cover and keep warm.

For sauce, bring pan juices to boiling. Boil gently, uncovered, stirring occasionally, about 10 minutes or till sauce is reduced to ⅔ cup (see photo 4, page 23). Spoon sauce over chicken. If desired, serve with asparagus spears (see tip box below). Makes 4 servings.

Turmeric-Poached Chicken

Turmeric lends a pleasant golden color to the chicken during cooking.

2 whole medium chicken breasts
    (1½ pounds total), halved lengthwise
1⅓ cups water
1 stalk celery, cut up
1 teaspoon chili powder
½ teaspoon salt
¼ teaspoon turmeric
¼ teaspoon instant chicken bouillon granules
⅛ teaspoon pepper
    Steamed sliced zucchini (optional)

Pull skin off chicken breasts (see photo 1, page 76). Rinse chicken.

In a 10-inch skillet combine water, celery, chili powder, salt, turmeric, bouillon granules, and pepper. Bring to boiling. Carefully add chicken (see photo 1, page 22). Reduce heat, then cover and simmer for 15 minutes.

Turn chicken, then simmer 5 to 10 minutes more or till tender (see photo 5, page 35). Use a slotted spoon to transfer chicken to a serving platter. If desired, serve with zucchini (see tip box below). Makes 4 servings.

Steaming Vegetables

Steamed vegetables are a perfect accompaniment to poached poultry. They add color that is eye-pleasing and texture that is palate-pleasing!

Begin by washing the vegetables thoroughly. For the asparagus served with Curry- and Wine-Sauced Chicken, scrape off the scales and break off the woody bases. For the zucchini served with Turmeric-Poached Chicken, simply cut off the ends and slice it. *Do not peel.*

Place the vegetables in a steamer basket. Put basket over (not touching) boiling water in a saucepan. Cover. Reduce heat. Steam till tender, 13 to 18 minutes for asparagus or 8 to 13 minutes for zucchini.

Simple Chicken Salads

Light, refreshing, and just right for a summer luncheon or supper. That's a perfect description of these delicately seasoned chicken salads.

Tossed with succulent fruit or crisp vegetables and topped with a delightful dressing, these salads are just the right size to satisfy without over-stuffing. Make them ahead so lunch is ready when you are.

Cantaloupe Chicken Salad

Cantaloupe Chicken Salad

 2 medium cantaloupe, chilled
 ⅓ cup mayonnaise *or* salad dressing
 ¼ cup dairy sour cream
 2 teaspoons soy sauce
 ½ teaspoon ground ginger
 ⅛ teaspoon pepper
 2 whole medium chicken breasts
   (1½ pounds total), halved lengthwise,
   cooked and chilled (see page 24)
 ½ cup sliced celery
 ½ cup fresh pea pods, cut crosswise into
   thirds
 ¼ cup toasted sliced almonds
   Lettuce leaves (optional)

Use a sawtooth cut to halve cantaloupe (see photo 1). Remove seeds. Leaving a ¾-inch-wide rim around the top of each half, scoop out fruit. Scoop from underneath rim, leaving a ¼- to ½-inch shell inside melon (see photo 2). Reserve *3 cups* of the melon pieces for salad; store any remaining for another use.

In a small mixing bowl stir together mayonnaise or salad dressing, sour cream, soy sauce, ginger, and pepper (see photo 3). Set aside.

Remove meat from chicken breast bones; cube meat (see photo 4).

In a large mixing bowl combine reserved melon pieces, chicken, celery, and pea pods. Add mayonnaise mixture, then toss to coat. Chill, if desired. To serve, spoon about *1¼ cups* filling into *each* melon shell. Top *each* shell with *1 tablespoon* almonds. If desired, serve on lettuce-lined plates. Makes 4 servings.

1 To make a sawtooth cut, use a toothpick to mark the top and bottom point of each sawtooth just above and below the center of the cantaloupe. Make the marks ½ inch apart. Insert a paring knife diagonally between an adjacent top and bottom mark, pushing the knife into the center of the cantaloupe, as shown. Repeat cutting between all marks; pull the halves apart.

2 Leaving a ¾-inch-wide rim around the top edge of each melon half, use a melon baller to scoop out the fruit and shape it into balls. Scoop the balls from underneath the rim, leaving a ¼- to ½-inch shell inside the melon. (*Or,* use a spoon to scoop out the fruit, then use a knife to cube it.) The rim around the top helps create an attractive shell.

3 Stir the mayonnaise mixture with a wire whisk or spoon, as shown, till the seasonings are evenly distributed. If you like, make the dressing ahead of time and chill it. Stir it again before using.

4 With the chicken bone-side up, loosen the meat from the breast bones and pull the bones away. Discard the bones. Cube the meat by cutting it into pieces that measure ½ inch on each side.

Chicken and Brown Rice in Tomatoes

When cooked, brown rice triples in volume; ½ cup uncooked brown rice measures 1½ cups when cooked.

  4 **large tomatoes**
  ½ **cup mayonnaise *or* salad dressing**
  3 **tablespoons Italian salad dressing**
  ¼ **teaspoon salt**
  ⅛ **teaspoon pepper**
  2 **whole medium chicken breasts (1½ pounds total), halved lengthwise, cooked and chilled (see page 24)**
1½ **cups cooked brown rice**
  ⅓ **cup sliced pitted ripe olives**
  ¼ **cup sliced green onion**
     Lettuce leaves
     Snipped parsley

Remove tomato cores. Starting at stem end, cut each tomato into 6 wedges, cutting to, but not through, base of tomato. Spread wedges apart, then season lightly with salt. Cover and chill.

In a small mixing bowl stir together mayonnaise or salad dressing, Italian dressing, ¼ teaspoon salt, and pepper (see photo 3, page 29).

Remove meat from chicken breast bones; cube meat (see photo 4, page 29).

In a large mixing bowl combine chicken, rice, ripe olives, and green onion. Add mayonnaise mixture, then toss to coat. Chill, if desired.

To serve, line 4 individual salad plates with lettuce leaves. Carefully place a tomato on each. Spoon about *1 cup* salad into the center of spread wedges of *each* tomato. Sprinkle with parsley. Makes 4 servings.

Chicken Macaroni Salad

Mustard adds tongue-tingling hotness.

  ¾ **cup medium shell *or* elbow macaroni**
  ½ **cup green goddess salad dressing**
  2 **tablespoons milk**
  2 **teaspoons Dijon-style mustard**
     Dash pepper
  2 **whole medium chicken breasts (1½ pounds total), halved lengthwise, cooked and chilled (see page 24)**
  ½ **cup shredded carrots**
  ½ **cup finely chopped broccoli flowerets**
  ¼ **cup chopped green pepper**
     Lettuce *or* cabbage leaves

In a large saucepan cook macaroni in a large amount of boiling salted water till tender; drain. Rinse with cold water; drain well. Set aside.

In a small mixing bowl stir together green goddess salad dressing, milk, mustard, and pepper (see photo 3, page 29).

Remove meat from chicken breast bones; cube meat (see photo 4, page 29).

In a large mixing bowl combine macaroni, chicken, carrots, broccoli, and green pepper. Add dressing mixture, then toss to coat. Cover and chill in the refrigerator for 1 hour.

To serve, line 3 salad bowls or salad plates with lettuce or cabbage leaves. Spoon *1⅓ cups* salad onto *each*. Makes 3 servings.

Peachy Chicken-Filled Pitas

Pita bread is also called pocket bread because its two halves open up, forming a pocket—a great place to tuck a first-rate filling!

½ cup plain yogurt
¼ teaspoon ground cinnamon
⅛ teaspoon salt
2 whole medium chicken breasts
    (1½ pounds total), halved lengthwise,
    cooked and chilled (see page 24)
2 medium peaches, peeled, pitted, and
    chopped *or* one 8¾-ounce can peach
    slices, drained and chopped
⅓ cup chopped celery
¼ cup chopped pecans
4 large pita bread rounds, halved
    crosswise
    Spinach leaves *or* alfalfa sprouts

In a small mixing bowl stir together yogurt, cinnamon, and salt (see photo 3, page 29).

Remove meat from chicken breast bones; cube meat (see photo 4, page 29).

In a large mixing bowl combine chicken, peaches, celery, and pecans. Add yogurt mixture, then toss to coat. Chill, if desired. To serve, line each pita half with spinach leaves or alfalfa sprouts. Spoon about ⅓ cup filling into *each* pita half. Serve at once. Makes 4 servings.

Chicken Salad Croissants

½ cup frozen peas
½ cup mayonnaise *or* salad dressing
½ teaspoon dried dillweed, oregano
    or thyme, crushed
2 whole sweet pickles, chopped (¼ cup)
1 2-ounce jar diced pimiento, drained
2 whole medium chicken breasts
    (1½ pounds total), halved lengthwise,
    cooked and chilled (see page 24)
2 hard-cooked eggs, chilled and cut up
6 croissants *or* bagels, halved horizontally
    Leaf lettuce

Place peas in a colander and rinse under warm running water to thaw and separate.

In a small mixing bowl stir together mayonnaise or salad dressing; dillweed, oregano, or thyme; and ¼ teaspoon *salt* (see photo 3, page 29). Stir in peas, pickles, and pimiento.

Remove meat from chicken breast bones; cube meat (see photo 4, page 29).

In a large mixing bowl combine chicken and eggs. Add mayonnaise mixture, then toss to coat. Chill, if desired. To serve, line bottom halves of croissants or bagels with lettuce leaves. Spoon about ½ cup salad onto *each*. Replace top halves. Makes 6 servings.

You Can Use Canned Or Frozen Chicken

When you don't have time to cook fresh chicken for these salad recipes, use convenient canned or frozen chicken. Simply substitute two 5-ounce cans chunk-style chicken, chilled and drained, *or* 2 cups frozen diced cooked chicken, thawed, for 2 cooked and chilled whole medium chicken breasts (1½ pounds total).

Frying in The Oven

Love that crispy fried chicken, but wish there was a shortcut to making it? Well, there is. And it comes with less mess, fewer calories, and more ease to boot.

The technique is known as oven frying—one of the top ten best secrets in cooking. The crisp crunch of these chicken pieces will never reveal your easy way of frying.

Cheesy Caraway Chicken

Cheesy Caraway Chicken

1½ cups bite-size cheese crackers
1 teaspoon caraway seed
¼ teaspoon pepper
2 whole medium chicken breasts (1½ pounds total), halved lengthwise
2 tablespoons milk
Kale (optional)

Place crackers in a plastic bag, then use a rolling pin to crush (see photo 1). Transfer to a pie plate or shallow bowl. Stir in caraway seed and pepper. Set aside.

Rinse chicken, then pat dry. Brush chicken with milk (see photo 2). Coat with crumb mixture (see photo 3). Place, skin side up, in an un-greased 13x9x2-inch baking pan (see photo 4).

Bake in a 375° oven 45 to 55 minutes or till tender (see photo 5). Transfer to a platter. If desired, garnish with kale. Makes 4 servings.

1 Place the crackers in a plastic bag, leaving the end open so air can escape. Roll a rolling pin over the bag, crushing the crackers, as shown. *Or,* crush the crackers by pressing them against the counter with the palm of your hand, or by squeezing the bag in your hands. Crushing the crackers in a plastic bag saves cleanup.

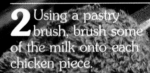

2 Using a pastry brush, brush some of the milk onto each chicken piece.

3 Roll the chicken pieces in the crumb mixture, patting to coat each side evenly.

4 Place the chicken, skin side up, in the ungreased baking pan. Make sure the pieces do not touch each other or the sides of the pan.

5 The chicken is done when it is tender enough to be easily pierced with a fork. Also, the juices should run clear, not pink.

Crisp Chip Chicken

Eating this crispy, crunchy chicken is only half the fun; try saying the recipe name fast three times in a row.

2 **cups potato chips**
1½ **cups crisp rice cereal**
¼ **teaspoon ground red pepper**
1 **beaten egg**
¼ **cup milk**
1 **2½- to 3-pound broiler-fryer chicken, cut-up (see pages 120-121)**

Place potato chips and cereal in a plastic bag, then use a hand to crush (see photo 1, page 34). Transfer mixture to a pie plate, then stir in red pepper. Set aside.

In a shallow mixing bowl or pie plate stir together egg and milk. Rinse chicken, then pat dry. Dip chicken into egg mixture. Coat with chip mixture (see photo 3, page 34). Place chicken, skin side up, in an ungreased 15x10x1-inch baking pan (see photo 4, page 35).

Bake in a 375° oven for 45 to 55 minutes or till tender (see photo 5, page 35). Transfer to a platter. Makes 6 servings.

Oven-Fried Potato And Herb Chicken

A clever way of combining meat and potato flavors in a single dish!

1 **cup instant mashed potato flakes**
1 **teaspoon paprika**
1 **teaspoon dried tarragon *or* thyme, crushed**
½ **teaspoon salt**
⅛ **teaspoon garlic powder**
⅛ **teaspoon pepper**
1 **2½- to 3-pound broiler-fryer chicken, cut up (see pages 120-121)**
2 **tablespoons milk**

Place potato flakes in a pie plate or shallow mixing bowl. Stir in paprika, tarragon or thyme, salt, garlic powder, and pepper. Set aside.

Rinse chicken, then pat dry. Brush chicken with milk (see photo 2, page 34). Coat with potato flake mixture (see photo 3, page 34). Place chicken, skin side up, in an ungreased 15x10x1-inch baking pan (see photo 4, page 35).

Bake in a 375° oven for 45 to 55 minutes or till tender (see photo 5, page 35). Transfer to a platter. Makes 6 servings.

Cutting Up Cut-Up Chicken

A package of cut-up chicken isn't necessarily cut up—not completely, anyway. Often the drumsticks still need to be divided from the thighs, and sometimes the breast needs to be split.
To help you finish cutting up your chicken, refer to the directions given on pages 120 and 121.

Soy-Sesame Oven-Fried Chicken

Sesame seed are easy to toast, and the rich flavor that results is well worth the time. Simply place them in a pie plate and bake in a 375° oven for 8 to 10 minutes; stir once or twice. Check the seeds at 8 minutes—once they start to brown, they finish browning quite quickly.

¼ cup sesame seed, toasted
2 whole medium chicken breasts
(1½ pounds total), halved lengthwise
2 tablespoons soy sauce
1 teaspoon five-spice powder *or*
Homemade Five-Spice Powder*

Place sesame seed in a pie plate. Set aside.

Rinse chicken, then pat dry. In a small mixing bowl combine soy sauce and five-spice powder. Brush chicken with soy mixture (see photo 2, page 34). Coat skin side with sesame seed (see photo 3, page 34). Place chicken, skin side up, in an ungreased 13x9x2-inch baking dish (see photo 4, page 35).

Bake in a 375° oven for 45 to 55 minutes or till tender (see photo 5, page 35). Transfer to a platter. Makes 6 servings.

*Homemade Five-Spice Powder:** In a small mixing bowl combine 1 teaspoon ground *cinnamon;* 1 teaspoon crushed *aniseed or* 1 *star anise*, ground; ¼ teaspoon crushed *fennel seed;* ¼ teaspoon freshly ground *pepper* or ¼ teaspoon *Szechuan pepper;* and ⅛ teaspoon ground *cloves.* Store in a covered container. Makes about 3 teaspoons.

Indian-Style Oven-Fried Chicken

It's the coating—curry powder, red pepper, peanuts, and coconut—that gives the chicken a Far East aura.

2 tablespoons butter *or* margarine
1½ teaspoons curry powder
¼ teaspoon ground red pepper
½ cup dry roasted peanuts
⅓ cup coconut
¼ cup yellow cornmeal
1 teaspoon paprika
¼ teaspoon salt
1 2½- to 3-pound broiler-fryer chicken, cut up (see pages 120-121)

In a small saucepan melt butter or margarine over medium heat. Stir in curry powder and red pepper. Cook and stir for 1 minute. Set aside.

In a blender container or a food processor combine peanuts and coconut. Blend or process till peanuts are ground. Transfer mixture to a pie plate or shallow mixing bowl. Stir in cornmeal, paprika, and salt. Set aside.

Rinse chicken; pat dry. Brush chicken with butter mixture (see photo 2, page 34). Coat with peanut mixture (see photo 3, page 34). Place chicken, skin side up, in an ungreased 15x10x1-inch baking pan (see photo 4, page 35).

Bake in a 375° oven for 45 to 55 minutes or till tender (see photo 5, page 35). Transfer to a platter. Makes 6 servings.

Crispy Pan-Frying

If there's one food that's ever-popular with most people, it has to be the famous home-style fried chicken. Whether it's served crispy hot at the family table or simply chilled at an outdoor picnic, it's always a big hit.

Choose from our wide variety of both familiar and creative coatings. We're sure you'll find one that leaves your taste buds dancing.

Crispy Chicken Fiesta Platter

Crispy Chicken Fiesta Platter

¼ **cup all-purpose flour**
2 **teaspoons chili powder**
¼ **teaspoon garlic powder**
¼ **teaspoon ground red pepper**
1 **2½- to 3-pound broiler-fryer chicken,**
  cut up (see pages 120-121)
2 **tablespoons cooking oil *or* shortening**
1 **cup shredded lettuce**
1 **tomato, cut into wedges**
  Tortilla chips

In a plastic or paper bag combine flour, chili powder, garlic powder, red pepper, and ½ teaspoon *salt*. Rinse chicken, then pat dry. Add chicken, 2 or 3 pieces at a time, to the bag, then shake to coat (see photo 1).

In a 12-inch skillet heat oil or shortening. Add chicken (see photo 2).

Cook, uncovered, over medium-low heat 50 to 60 minutes or till tender (see photo 5, page 35). Turn occasionally (see photo 3). Remove chicken, then drain on paper towels.

Arrange lettuce, tomato, and tortilla chips on a platter. Place chicken on top. Garnish with a jalapeño pepper, if desired. Serves 6.

Fried Chicken Fiesta Platter: Prepare Crispy Chicken Fiesta Platter as above, *except* cook, uncovered, over medium heat 10 to 15 minutes, turning to brown evenly (see photo 3). Reduce heat, then cover tightly. Cook 30 minutes. Uncover, then cook 5 to 10 minutes more or till tender (see photo 5, page 35). Remove chicken, then drain on paper towels.

Easy Chicken Fiesta Platter: Prepare Crispy Chicken Fiesta Platter as above, *except* use a 12-inch ovenproof skillet (see tip box, page 43). Cook chicken, uncovered, over medium heat 10 to 15 minutes, turning to brown evenly (see photo 3). Drain off fat. Transfer skillet to a 375° oven (see photo 4). Bake, uncovered, 30 to 35 minutes or till tender (see photo 5, page 35). *Do not turn during baking.*

1 Combine the flour and seasonings in a plastic or paper bag. Add 2 or 3 chicken pieces to the bag. Close the bag, then shake to coat the pieces evenly with the flour mixture.

2 Place the meaty pieces of chicken (breast halves, thighs, and large ends of drumsticks) toward the center of the skillet where the heat is most intense. Place the remaining pieces toward the edge.

3 Cook the chicken over medium-low heat, turning occasionally in order to brown the chicken evenly, as shown. Chicken is done when it is tender enough to be easily pierced with a fork.

4 Chicken may be partially cooked on the range top, then finished in the oven. Simply use an ovenproof skillet (see tip box, page 43). Cook the chicken 10 to 15 minutes. Drain the fat; transfer skillet to a 375° oven, as shown. (*Or*, remove the chicken from the skillet and place, skin side up, in an ungreased large shallow baking pan.)

Hawaiian-Style Fried Chicken

A heavenly blend of tropical fruit, nuts, and spices.

¼ **cup all-purpose flour**
2 **teaspoons brown sugar**
½ **teaspoon salt**
½ **teaspoon dry mustard**
¼ **teaspoon ground ginger**
⅛ **teaspoon pepper**
2 **whole medium chicken breasts
(1½ pounds total), halved lengthwise**
2 **tablespoons cooking oil *or* shortening**
⅔ **cup long grain rice**
⅓ **cup macadamia nuts *or* cashews,
chopped and toasted**
1 **15¼-ounce can pineapple tidbits
(juice pack)**
¼ **cup chopped green pepper**
1 **tablespoon butter *or* margarine**
1 **tablespoon cornstarch**
1 **teaspoon brown sugar**
½ **teaspoon dry mustard**
1 **tablespoon soy sauce**

In a plastic or paper bag combine flour, 2 teaspoons brown sugar, salt, ½ teaspoon dry mustard, ginger, and pepper. Rinse chicken; pat dry. Add chicken, 2 or 3 pieces at a time, to the bag, then shake to coat (see photo 1, page 40).

In a 10-inch skillet heat oil or shortening. Add chicken (see photo 2, page 40).

Cook, uncovered, over medium heat 10 to 15 minutes, turning to brown evenly (see photo 3, page 41). Reduce heat, then cover tightly. Cook 25 minutes. Uncover, then cook 5 to 10 minutes more or till chicken is tender (see photo 5, page 35). Remove chicken; drain on paper towels.

Meanwhile, in a medium saucepan combine rice and 1⅓ cups *water*. Bring to boiling. Reduce heat, then cover and simmer 15 minutes. *Do not lift cover.* Remove from heat. Let stand, covered, 10 minutes. Stir in nuts.

For pineapple sauce, drain pineapple, reserving juice. Set aside. In a medium saucepan cook green pepper in hot butter or margarine till tender but not brown. Stir in cornstarch, 1 teaspoon brown sugar, and ½ teaspoon dry mustard. Add reserved juice and soy sauce. Cook and stir till thickened and bubbly, then cook and stir 2 minutes more. Stir in pineapple.

To serve, transfer rice to a serving platter. Top with chicken and pineapple sauce. Serves 4.

Herbed Fried Chicken

Here's a recipe for fried chicken that's nicely herby!

½ **cup fine dry bread crumbs**
1 **tablespoon dried parsley flakes**
½ **teaspoon salt**
½ **teaspoon dried thyme, crushed**
½ **teaspoon dried marjoram, crushed**
¼ **teaspoon dried rosemary, crushed**
¼ **teaspoon pepper**
1 **2½- to 3-pound broiler-fryer chicken,
cut up (see pages 120-121)**
2 **tablespoons cooking oil *or* shortening**

In a plastic or paper bag combine bread crumbs, parsley, salt, thyme, marjoram, rosemary, and pepper. Rinse chicken, then pat dry. Add chicken, 2 or 3 pieces at a time, to the bag, then shake to coat (see photo 1, page 40).

In a 12-inch skillet heat oil or shortening. Add chicken (see photo 2, page 40).

Cook, uncovered, over medium heat 10 to 15 minutes, turning to brown evenly (see photo 3, page 41). Reduce heat, then cover tightly. Cook 30 minutes. Uncover, then cook 5 to 10 minutes more or till tender (see photo 5, page 35). Remove chicken; drain on paper towels. Serves 6.

Crusty Cornmeal Chicken Thighs

These "corny" thighs don't need your attention during the last ½ hour of cooking as many fried chicken recipes do.

¼ **cup all-purpose flour**
¼ **cup yellow cornmeal**
2 **tablespoons toasted wheat germ**
½ **teaspoon salt**
½ **teaspoon dried thyme, crushed**
6 **chicken thighs (1¾ pounds total)**
2 **tablespoons lemon juice**
2 **tablespoons cooking oil *or* shortening**

In a pie plate combine flour, cornmeal, wheat germ, salt, thyme, and ⅛ teaspoon *pepper.* Rinse chicken; pat dry. Brush with lemon juice. Coat with flour mixture (see photo 3, page 34).

In a 10-inch ovenproof skillet heat oil or shortening. Add chicken (see photo 2, page 40).

Cook, uncovered, over medium heat 10 to 15 minutes, turning to brown evenly (see photo 3, page 41). Drain off fat.

Transfer the skillet to a 375° oven (see photo 4, page 41). Bake, uncovered, 30 to 35 minutes or till tender (see photo 5, page 35). *Do not turn chicken during baking.* Makes 6 servings.

Improvising an Ovenproof Skillet

Perhaps you don't own an ovenproof skillet, but want to make a recipe that calls for one. Simply wrap your skillet's handle in several layers of aluminum foil. This will protect that handle from the intense oven heat.

Down-Home Fried Chicken

Our fantastic version of southern-style fried chicken.

¼ **cup all-purpose flour**
1 **teaspoon paprika**
1 **teaspoon ground savory *or* poultry seasoning**
½ **teaspoon onion *or* garlic salt**
¼ **teaspoon pepper**
1 **2½- to 3-pound broiler-fryer chicken, cut up (see pages 120-121)**
2 **tablespoons cooking oil *or* shortening**

In a plastic or paper bag combine flour, paprika, savory or poultry seasoning, onion or garlic salt, and pepper. Rinse chicken, then pat dry. Add chicken, 2 or 3 pieces at a time, to the bag, then shake to coat (see photo 1, page 40).

In a 12-inch skillet heat oil or shortening. Add chicken (see photo 2, page 40).

Cook, uncovered, over medium-low heat 50 to 60 minutes or till tender (see photo 5, page 35). Turn occasionally (see photo 3, page 41). Remove chicken; drain on paper towels. Serves 6.

Covered Down-Home Chicken: Prepare Down-Home Fried Chicken as above, *except* cook, uncovered, over medium heat 10 to 15 minutes, turning to brown evenly (see photo 3, page 41). Reduce heat, then cover tightly. Cook 30 minutes. Uncover, then cook 5 to 10 minutes more or till tender (see photo 5, page 35). Remove chicken, then drain on paper towels.

Pan-in-the-Oven Down-Home Chicken: Prepare Down-Home Fried Chicken as above, *except* use a 12-inch ovenproof skillet (see tip box at left). Cook chicken, uncovered, over medium heat 10 to 15 minutes, turning to brown evenly (see photo 3, page 41). Drain off fat. Transfer the skillet to a 375° oven (see photo 4, page 41). Bake, uncovered, 30 to 35 minutes or till tender (see photo 5, page 35). *Do not turn chicken during baking.*

44

So-Easy Broiling

Here's an easy way to fix poultry just like it's hot off the grill. Simply step into your kitchen and turn on the broiler.

That's right—broiling and barbecuing are interchangeable because both cook with direct heat. In broiling, the heat simply comes from above, and in barbecuing, it comes from below.

Though broiling is handy for a rainy day, don't wait for one to try our flavorfully glazed and perfectly broiled recipes.

Orange-Ginger Glazed Chicken

Orange-Ginger Glazed Chicken

2	**whole medium chicken breasts (1½ pounds total), halved lengthwise**
½	**cup orange marmalade**
2	**tablespoons sliced green onion**
2	**tablespoons vinegar**
1	**tablespoon soy sauce**
¼	**teaspoon ground ginger**
	Onion brushes (optional)
	Orange twists (optional)

Preheat the broiler. Rinse chicken, then pat dry. Season with salt and pepper. Place, skin side down, on a rack in an unheated broiler pan (see photo 1). Place under the broiler 5 to 6 inches from the heat (see photo 2). Broil about 20 minutes or till chicken is light brown.

Meanwhile, for glaze, in a small mixing bowl combine marmalade, green onion, vinegar, soy sauce, and ginger.

Turn chicken skin side up (see photo 3). Broil 10 to 20 minutes more or till chicken is tender (see photo 5, page 35). Brush with glaze the last 5 to 10 minutes (see photo 4). Transfer to a serving platter, then brush on any remaining glaze. Garnish with onion brushes and orange twists, if desired. Makes 4 servings.

Grilled Orange-Ginger Glazed Chicken: Prepare Orange-Ginger Glazed Chicken as above, *except* place chicken, skin side down, on an uncovered grill, directly over *medium* coals for 20 minutes (see photos 1 and 3, pages 52 and 53). Turn chicken skin side up (see photo 3). Grill 10 to 20 minutes more or till chicken is tender (see photo 5, page 35). Brush with glaze the last 5 to 10 minutes (see photo 4).

1 Preheat the broiler unit before cooking. *Don't* preheat the broiler pan and rack. (Preheating the pan and rack could cause them to warp and may also cause the chicken to stick.) Place the chicken, skin side down, on the *unheated* rack.

2 Place the broiler pan and rack under the heating unit so the surface of the chicken is 5 to 6 inches from the heating unit. Use a ruler to measure this 5- to 6-inch distance.

For units that don't allow 5 to 6 inches between the heating unit and food, remove the rack from the broiler pan. Set the chicken in the bottom of the pan to compensate for the distance.

3 When the chicken is light brown on the first side (this takes about 20 minutes), use tongs to turn the pieces skin side up.

4 Brush the glaze onto the chicken pieces only during the last 5 to 10 minutes of broiling to avoid burning the glaze. Brush any remaining glaze on the chicken pieces after they have been placed on a serving platter.

Barbecue-Style Broiled Drumsticks

8 **chicken drumsticks *or* thighs (2¼ pounds total)**
¼ **cup catsup**
2 **tablespoons vinegar**
2 **tablespoons water**
1 **teaspoon brown sugar**
1 **teaspoon Worcestershire sauce**
½ **teaspoon chili powder**
¼ **teaspoon dry mustard**
  Dash bottled hot pepper sauce

Preheat the broiler. Rinse chicken, then pat dry. Place chicken, skin side down, on a rack in an unheated broiler pan (see photo 1, page 46). Place under the broiler 5 to 6 inches from the heat (see photo 2, page 46). Broil about 20 minutes or till chicken is light brown.

Meanwhile, for sauce, in a small saucepan stir together catsup, vinegar, water, brown sugar, Worcestershire sauce, chili powder, dry mustard, and hot pepper sauce. Bring to boiling. Reduce heat; simmer, uncovered, 10 minutes.

Turn chicken skin side up (see photo 3, page 47). Broil 10 to 20 minutes more or till tender (see photo 5, page 35). Brush with sauce the last 5 to 10 minutes (see photo 4, page 47). Transfer to a serving platter, then brush on any remaining sauce. Makes 4 servings.

Apple Broiled Chicken

A simple, sweet glaze with just a hint of mustard flavor.

1 **2½- to 3-pound broiler-fryer chicken, cut up (see pages 120-121)**
¼ **cup apple jelly**
½ **teaspoon prepared mustard**
¼ **teaspoon dried rosemary, crushed**

Preheat the broiler. Rinse chicken, then pat dry. Season with salt and pepper. Place, skin side down, on a rack in an unheated broiler pan (see photo 1, page 46). Place under the broiler 5 to 6 inches from the heat (see photo 2, page 46). Broil about 20 minutes or till light brown.

Meanwhile, for glaze, in a small saucepan combine apple jelly, mustard, and rosemary. Cook and stir till jelly is melted.

Turn chicken skin side up (see photo 3, page 47). Broil 10 to 20 minutes more or till tender (see photo 5, page 35). Brush with glaze the last 2 minutes (see photo 4, page 47). Transfer to a serving platter, then brush on any remaining glaze. Makes 6 servings.

Barbecued Variations

Because broiling and barbecuing are similar methods of cooking, any of these broiled recipes also may be barbecued. Simply prepare the recipe as directed, *except* place chicken, skin side down, on an uncovered grill, directly over *medium* coals for 20 minutes (see photos 1 and 3, pages 52 and 53). Turn chicken skin side up (see photo 3, page 47). Grill for 10 to 20 minutes more or till tender (see photo 5, page 35). Brush with sauce, glaze, or butter mixture during the last few minutes of cooking time as directed in the recipe (see photo 4, page 47).

Spicy Cherry-Sauced Chicken

Stir lemon and spices into a jar of cherry preserves for an easy, tasty sauce.

1 2½- to 3-pound broiler-fryer chicken, cut up (see pages 120-121)
1 12-ounce jar cherry preserves
1 tablespoon butter *or* margarine
½ teaspoon finely shredded lemon peel
3 tablespoons lemon juice
½ teaspoon ground cinnamon
¼ teaspoon ground allspice
⅛ teaspoon salt
⅛ teaspoon ground cloves
   Lemon slices (optional)

Preheat the broiler. Rinse chicken, then pat dry. Season with salt and pepper. Place, skin side down, on a rack in an unheated broiler pan (see photo 1, page 46). Place under the broiler 5 to 6 inches from the heat (see photo 2, page 46). Broil about 20 minutes or till light brown.

Meanwhile, for sauce, in a small saucepan combine preserves, butter or margarine, lemon peel, lemon juice, cinnamon, allspice, salt, and cloves. Cook and stir till well combined.

Turn chicken skin side up (see photo 3, page 47). Broil 10 to 20 minutes more or till tender (see photo 5, page 35). Brush with sauce the last 5 to 10 minutes (see photo 4, page 47). Transfer to a serving platter, then brush with sauce. Garnish with lemon slices, if desired. Pass any remaining sauce. Makes 4 servings.

Savory-Butter Broiled Chicken

The herb butter mixture keeps the breast meat moist and juicy.

2 whole medium chicken breasts (1½ pounds total), halved lengthwise
2 tablespoons butter *or* margarine, melted
2 teaspoons lemon juice
½ teaspoon dried savory, crushed
¼ teaspoon pepper
1 lemon, cut into wedges (optional)

Preheat the broiler. Rinse chicken, then pat dry. Season with salt and pepper. Place, skin side down, on a rack in an unheated broiler pan (see photo 1, page 46). Place under the broiler 5 to 6 inches from the heat (see photo 2, page 46). Broil about 20 minutes or till light brown.

Meanwhile, in a small bowl combine butter or margarine, lemon juice, savory, and pepper.

Turn chicken skin side up (see photo 3, page 47). Broil 10 to 20 minutes more or till tender (see photo 5, page 35). Brush with butter mixture the last 5 to 10 minutes (see photo 4, page 47). Transfer to a serving platter, then brush on any remaining butter mixture. Garnish with lemon wedges, if desired. Makes 4 servings.

Barbecuing To Perfection

Ah! There's nothing quite like food prepared in the great outdoors. Somehow it just seems to taste better.

Our barbecued poultry recipes are no exception. Their snappy marinades and tasty sauces will leave your taste buds longing for more hot-off-the-grill specialties.

Hickory-Smoked Chicken Halves

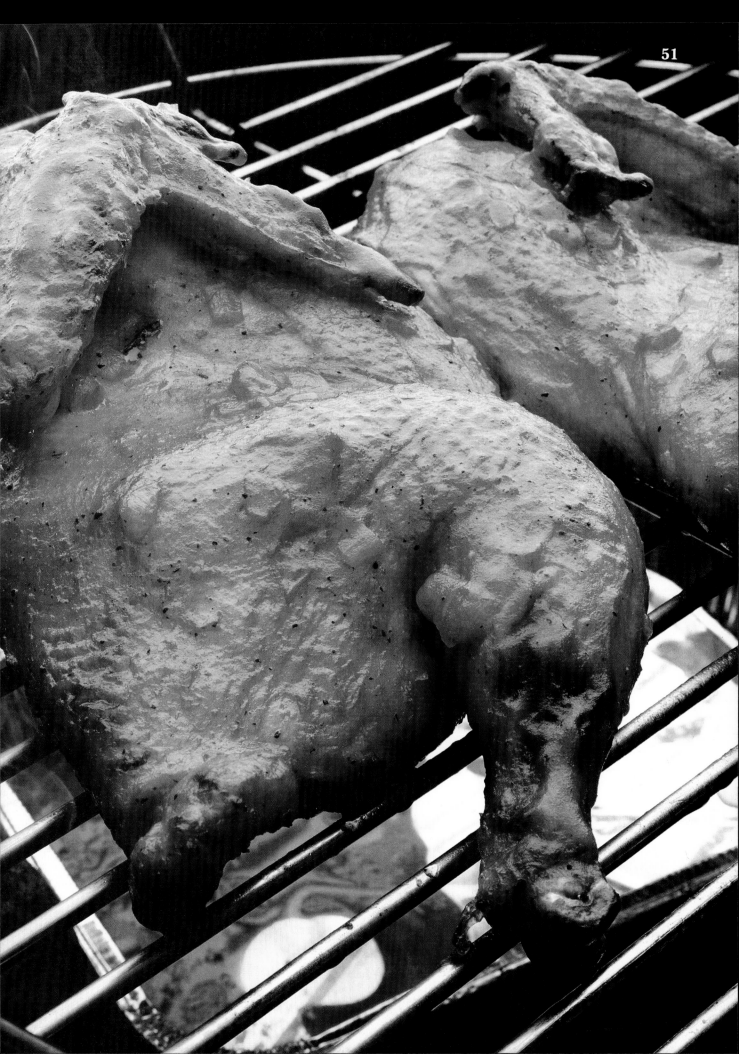

Hickory-Smoked Chicken Halves

We smoked our chicken with hickory chips, but alder, mesquite, oak, or osage orange chips work equally well.

4	cups hickory wood chips
2	tablespoons finely chopped onion
1	tablespoon butter *or* margarine
2	teaspoons cornstarch
½	cup tomato sauce
2	tablespoons vinegar
1	tablespoon honey
½	teaspoon dry mustard
¼	teaspoon salt
¼	teaspoon pepper
1	2½- to 3-pound broiler-fryer chicken

About 1 hour before cooking, soak hickory chips in enough water to cover.

In a covered grill mound the briquettes; ignite (see photo 1). When ready, arrange the coals in a circle leaving the center open; insert a foil drip pan (see photo 2). Test for *medium* coals (4-second count) over the drip pan (see photo 3).

Meanwhile, for sauce, in a small saucepan cook onion in hot butter or margarine till tender but not brown. Stir in cornstarch. Add tomato sauce, vinegar, honey, dry mustard, salt, and pepper. Cook and stir till thickened and bubbly, then cook and stir 2 minutes more.

Halve chicken (see photo 4). Rinse chicken, then pat dry. Season with salt and pepper. Drain hickory chips, then sprinkle *half* over the coals (see photo 5). Place chicken on the grill, skin side up, over the drip pan. Brush with sauce. Cover and grill 30 minutes. Brush with sauce and add remaining chips; grill 25 to 35 minutes more or till done (see photo 4, page 9). Transfer to a serving platter; brush with sauce. Pass remaining sauce. Makes 6 servings.

2 When the briquettes look ash gray, use long-handled tongs to arrange the coals in a circle, leaving the center open, as shown. Place a drip pan in the center. Use a purchased foil pan or make one using a double thickness of 18-inch-wide *heavy* foil.

1 In a covered charcoal grill, pile the briquettes into a pyramid-shape mound in the center of the firebox. Squirt briquettes with starter fluid, wait 1 minute, and carefully ignite with a long match, as shown. *Or,* use an electric fire starter to ignite the briquettes.

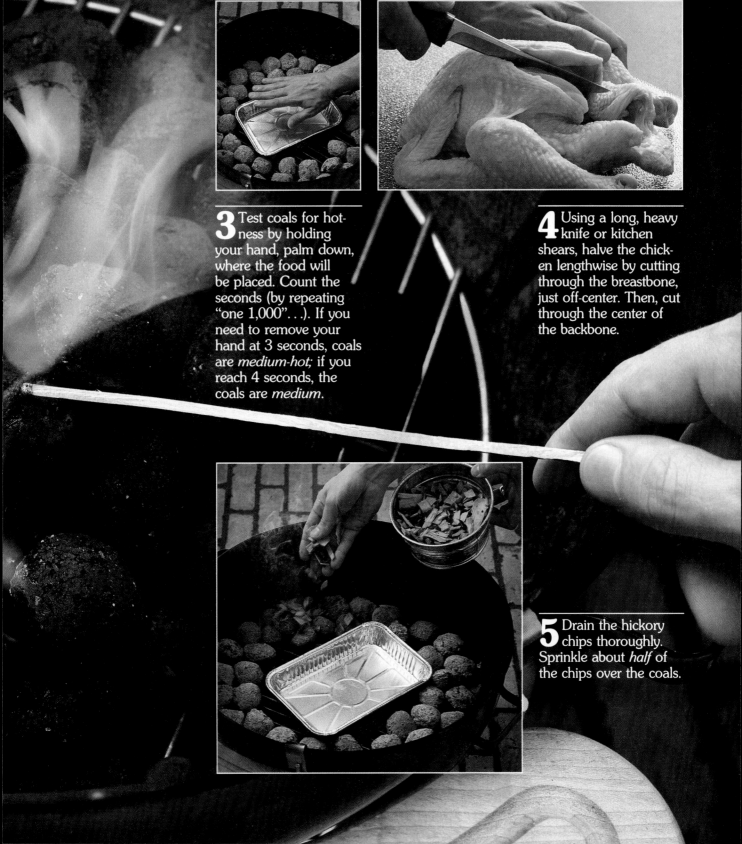

3 Test coals for hotness by holding your hand, palm down, where the food will be placed. Count the seconds (by repeating "one 1,000"...). If you need to remove your hand at 3 seconds, coals are *medium-hot;* if you reach 4 seconds, the coals are *medium.*

4 Using a long, heavy knife or kitchen shears, halve the chicken lengthwise by cutting through the breastbone, just off-center. Then, cut through the center of the backbone.

5 Drain the hickory chips thoroughly. Sprinkle about *half* of the chips over the coals.

Chicken-Vegetable Kabobs

½ **cup chicken broth**
1 **small onion, sliced**
2 **tablespoons sugar**
1 **tablespoon cooking oil**
5 **whole black peppers**
4 **juniper berries**
4 **whole cloves**
2 **bay leaves**
½ **cup white wine vinegar**
2 **boneless medium chicken breasts
   (1 pound total)**
½ **pound whole tiny new potatoes**
2 **medium carrots, bias-sliced into
   1-inch lengths**
1 **9-ounce package frozen artichoke hearts**

For marinade, in a small saucepan stir together chicken broth, onion, sugar, oil, peppers, juniper berries, cloves, bay leaves, and ½ teaspoon *salt*. Bring to boiling. Reduce heat, then cover and simmer for 10 minutes. Remove from heat. Stir in vinegar. Cool for 30 minutes.

Rinse chicken, then pat dry. Cut into 2x1-inch strips. Place in a medium mixing bowl. Pour marinade over. Cover, then let stand 1 hour at room temperature or 4 hours in the refrigerator.

Peel a strip from around center of each potato. Cook potatoes and carrots in a small amount of boiling water for 13 minutes. Add artichoke hearts; cook 7 minutes more. Drain, then cool.

In an uncovered grill mound the briquettes; ignite (see photo 1, page 52). When ready, spread the coals out. Test for *medium-hot* coals (3-second count) at the height food will be cooked (see photo 3, page 53).

Drain chicken, reserving marinade. Alternately thread chicken, potatoes, carrots, and artichoke hearts loosely onto 4 long skewers. Place on the grill for 7 minutes. Turn and brush with reserved marinade. Grill 6 to 7 minutes more or till chicken is tender (see photo 5, page 35). Serves 4.

Broiled Chicken-Vegetable Kabobs: Prepare Chicken-Vegetable Kabobs as above, *except* preheat the broiler instead of igniting the briquettes. Place kabobs in a single layer on a rack in an unheated broiler pan. Place under the broiler 5 to 6 inches from the heat (see photo 2, page 46). Broil 7 minutes. Turn and brush with reserved marinade. Broil 6 to 7 minutes more or till tender (see photo 5, page 35).

Italian Marinated Cornish Hens

2 **1- to 1½-pound Cornish game hens**
½ **cup dry white wine**
2 **tablespoons olive oil**
1 **teaspoon dried oregano, crushed**
1 **teaspoon dried basil, crushed**
2 **cloves garlic, minced**

Halve hens (see photo 4, page 53). Rinse hen halves. Place in a heavy plastic bag set in a large mixing bowl. For marinade, in a small mixing bowl combine wine, oil, oregano, basil, and garlic. Pour over hens in bag; seal bag. Marinate overnight in refrigerator; turn bag occasionally.

In a covered grill mound the briquettes; ignite (see photo 1, page 52). When ready, arrange the coals in a circle, leaving the center open; insert a foil drip pan (see photo 2, page 52). Test for *medium* coals (4-second count) over the drip pan (see photo 3, page 53).

Drain hens, reserving marinade. Place hens on grill, skin side up, over the drip pan. Cover and grill 40 to 50 minutes or till done (see photo 4, page 9). Brush occasionally with marinade. Makes 4 servings.

Italian Marinated Pheasant: Prepare Italian Marinated Cornish Hens as above, *except* substitute one 3-pound domestic *pheasant,* quartered, for the hens. Makes 6 servings.

Maple-Orange Barbecued Chicken

A blend of maple, orange, and mustard flavors makes a sensational-tasting sauce.

2 tablespoons Dijon-style mustard
1 teaspoon finely shredded orange peel
½ teaspoon seasoned salt
½ teaspoon lemon pepper
½ cup orange juice
⅓ cup maple-flavored syrup
1 2½- to 3-pound broiler-fryer chicken, cut up (see pages 120-121)

In an uncovered grill mound the briquettes; ignite (see photo 1, page 52). When ready, spread the coals out. Test for *medium* coals (4-second count) at the height the food will be cooked (see photo 3, page 53).

Meanwhile, for sauce, in a small saucepan combine mustard, orange peel, seasoned salt, and lemon pepper. Gradually add orange juice and syrup, stirring till well combined. Bring to boiling. Reduce heat, then simmer, uncovered, 10 to 15 minutes or to desired consistency.

Rinse chicken, then pat dry. Season with salt and pepper. Place chicken on grill, skin side down, for 20 minutes. Turn chicken, skin side up. Grill 10 to 20 minutes more or till tender (see photo 5, page 35). Brush with sauce the last 5 to 10 minutes. Transfer to a serving platter; brush with any remaining sauce. Serves 6.

Maple-Orange Broiled Chicken: Prepare Maple-Orange Barbecued Chicken as above, *except* preheat the broiler instead of igniting the briquettes. Place chicken, skin side down, on a rack in an unheated broiler pan. Place under the broiler 5 to 6 inches from the heat (see photo 2, page 46). Broil about 20 minutes or till light brown. Turn skin side up. Broil 10 to 20 minutes more or till tender (see photo 5, page 35). Brush with sauce the last 5 to 10 minutes.

Teriyaki Turkey Thigh

1 2-pound turkey thigh *or* 4 chicken thighs (1¼ pounds total)
3 tablespoons soy sauce
1 tablespoon dry sherry
1½ teaspoons cooking oil
½ teaspoon dry mustard
½ teaspoon grated gingerroot
1 small clove garlic, minced
⅛ teaspoon onion powder

Rinse poultry, then pat dry. Place in a heavy plastic bag set in a large mixing bowl. For marinade, in a small mixing bowl combine soy sauce, sherry, oil, mustard, gingerroot, garlic, onion powder, and 2 tablespoons *water*. Pour over meat in bag; seal bag. Marinate overnight in refrigerator; turn bag occasionally.

In a covered grill mound the briquettes; ignite (see photo 1, page 52). When ready, arrange the coals in a circle, leaving the center open; insert a foil drip pan (see photo 2, page 52). Test for *medium* coals (4-second count) over the drip pan (see photo 3, page 53).

Drain meat, reserving marinade. Place meat on grill, skin side up, over the drip pan. Cover and grill about 1¼ hours for turkey or about 55 minutes for chicken or till tender (see photo 5, page 35). Brush with marinade the last 10 minutes. Makes 4 servings.

Gas and Electric Grills

You can use these recipes with gas and electric grills, too. Check the manufacturer's instructions for starting the grill and adjusting the temperature.

Building On a Sauce

We've made leftover chicken and turkey as exciting as the meals they came from. How? By hiding them like secret treasures in the favorite family dishes in this section.

Each recipe starts with a simple white sauce. From there, these creations take off in a multitude of directions. You'll find everything from soups to casseroles—and all are tantalizingly good!

Tortellini with Cream Cheese Sauce

Tortellini with Cream Cheese Sauce

Start the sauce as soon as the pasta begins cooking so they'll be ready at the same time.

½ pound fresh asparagus, cut into 2-inch pieces, *or* one 8-ounce package frozen cut asparagus
6 ounces cheese tortellini *or* fettuccine
1 medium onion, sliced and separated into rings
1 cup sliced fresh mushrooms *or* one 2½-ounce jar sliced mushrooms, drained
1 clove garlic, minced
2 tablespoons butter *or* margarine
4 teaspoons all-purpose flour
½ teaspoon salt
½ teaspoon dried oregano, crushed
⅛ teaspoon pepper
1⅔ cups milk
1 3-ounce package cream cheese, cut up
1½ cups chopped cooked chicken *or* turkey, *or* frozen diced cooked chicken, thawed
¼ cup snipped parsley
2 tablespoons chopped pimiento

In a saucepan cook fresh asparagus, covered, in a small amount of boiling water 8 to 10 minutes or till done. (*Or,* cook frozen asparagus according to package directions.) Drain; set aside.

Meanwhile, cook tortellini or fettuccine according to package directions; drain (see photo 1).

For sauce, in a medium saucepan cook onion, mushrooms, and garlic in hot butter or margarine till tender but not brown. Stir in flour, salt, oregano, and pepper (see photo 2). Add milk (see photo 3). Cook and stir till thickened and bubbly, then cook and stir 1 minute more (see photo 4). Remove from heat.

Stir in cream cheese till melted. (Sauce will thicken.) Add asparagus, chicken or turkey, parsley, and pimiento; heat through. Serve immediately over hot pasta. Makes 4 servings.

1 Cook the pasta according to the directions on the package. Immediately drain by pouring the pasta and water into a colander set in a sink, as shown. Keep pasta warm by putting the colander over a pot of hot water and covering it.

2 Cook the vegetables and garlic in the hot butter or margarine till they are tender but not brown. (The onion will be translucent.) Stir in the flour, salt, oregano, and pepper, as shown.

3 Add the milk all at once to the flour-butter mixture in the saucepan. Stir together.

4 Cook and stir until the mixture becomes thick and bubbly. Then cook and stir one minute more to prevent the starchy taste that uncooked flour has. This extra minute of cooking is not necessary if the mixture will be cooked further (for example, if it's put in the oven).

Chicken Primavera

½ cup bias-sliced carrots
2 cups broccoli flowerets
8 ounces linguine *or* spaghetti
⅓ cup bias-sliced green onion
2 tablespoons butter *or* margarine
2 tablespoons all-purpose flour
½ teaspoon salt
Dash ground allspice
1½ cups milk
½ cup shredded Monterey Jack cheese (2 ounces)
1½ cups chopped cooked chicken *or* turkey
¼ cup snipped parsley

In a medium saucepan cook carrots, covered, in a small amount of boiling salted water for 10 minutes. Add broccoli; return to boiling. Reduce heat, then cover and cook 5 minutes more. Drain. Set aside. Meanwhile, cook linguine or spaghetti according to the package directions. Drain immediately (see photo 1, page 58).

For sauce, in a medium saucepan cook green onion in hot butter or margarine till tender but not brown. Stir in flour, salt, and allspice (see photo 2, page 59). Add milk (see photo 3, page 59). Cook and stir till thickened and bubbly, then cook and stir 1 minute more (see photo 4, page 59). Remove from heat.

Add cheese, then stir till melted. Stir in carrots, broccoli, chicken or turkey, and parsley. Cover and heat through. Serve immediately over hot pasta. Makes 4 servings.

Biscuit-Topped Turkey Pot Pie

1 10-ounce package frozen mixed vegetables
⅓ cup celery cut into ½-inch slices
1 small onion, chopped (⅓ cup)
¼ cup butter *or* margarine
⅓ cup all-purpose flour
¼ teaspoon dried marjoram, crushed
¼ teaspoon ground sage
2 cups chicken broth
1 cup milk
2 cups chopped cooked turkey *or* chicken
1 package (5) refrigerated biscuits

Cook mixed vegetables according to the package directions. Drain. Set aside.

In a large saucepan cook celery and onion in hot butter or margarine till tender but not brown. Stir in flour, marjoram, and sage (see photo 2, page 59). Add chicken broth and milk (see photo 3, page 59). Cook and stir till thickened and bubbly (see photo 4, page 59). Stir in mixed vegetables and turkey or chicken; heat through. Turn mixture into a 2-quart casserole.

Cut each biscuit into quarters. Arrange on top of the *hot* turkey mixture. Bake, uncovered, in a 400° oven about 15 minutes or until biscuits are light brown. Makes 6 servings.

Attention Microwave Owners

Recipes with microwave directions were tested in countertop microwave ovens that operate on 600 to 700 watts.

Times are approximate since microwave ovens vary by manufacturer.

Chicken Divan-Style

1　**10-ounce package frozen broccoli *or* asparagus spears**
2　**tablespoons butter *or* margarine**
3　**tablespoons all-purpose flour**
⅛　**teaspoon ground nutmeg**
1　**cup milk**
2　**teaspoons lemon juice**
½　**cup grated Parmesan cheese**
10　**ounces sliced cooked chicken *or* turkey**
4　**slices Muenster *or* Swiss cheese (4 ounces)**
　　Paprika

Prepare broccoli or asparagus spears according to the package directions. Drain. Arrange in a 10x6x2-inch baking dish. Set aside.

For sauce, in a medium saucepan melt butter or margarine. Stir in flour and nutmeg (see photo 2, page 59). Add milk (see photo 3, page 59). Cook and stir till thickened and bubbly (see photo 4, page 59). Stir in lemon juice.

Pour *half* of the sauce over broccoli or asparagus; sprinkle with *half* of the Parmesan cheese. Top with chicken or turkey and Muenster or Swiss cheese. Pour remaining sauce over all; sprinkle with remaining Parmesan cheese and paprika. Bake in a 350° oven about 20 minutes or till heated through. Makes 6 servings.

Microwave Directions: In a 10x6x2-inch baking dish combine broccoli or asparagus spears and 2 tablespoons *water*. Micro-cook, covered, on 100% power (HIGH) 5 to 7 minutes; give the dish a half-turn once during cooking. Let stand, covered, 3 minutes. Drain.

For sauce, in a 2-cup glass measuring cup cook butter or margarine, uncovered, 30 to 40 seconds or till melted. Stir in flour and nutmeg (see photo 2, page 59). Add milk (see photo 3, page 59). Cook, uncovered, 3 to 4 minutes or till thickened and bubbly (see photo 4, page 59). Stir after each minute. Stir in lemon juice.
Pour *half* of the sauce over broccoli or aspara-

gus; sprinkle with *half* of the Parmesan cheese. Top with chicken or turkey and cheese. Pour remaining sauce over all; sprinkle with remaining Parmesan cheese and paprika. Cook, covered with waxed paper, 6 to 7 minutes or till heated through; give dish a half-turn once during cooking. Let stand 5 minutes.

Chicken Soup Élégant

½　**cup chopped celery**
½　**cup sliced leek**
¼　**cup butter *or* margarine**
¼　**cup all-purpose flour**
1½　**cups chicken broth**
2　**cups milk**
1½　**cups chopped cooked chicken *or* turkey**
½　**cup dry white wine *or* chicken broth**
　　Dash white pepper

Cook celery and leek in hot butter or margarine till tender but not brown. Stir in flour (see photo 2, page 59). Add broth and milk (see photo 3, page 59). Cook and stir till slightly thickened and bubbly, then cook and stir 1 minute more (see photo 4, page 59). Stir in chicken or turkey, wine or broth, and pepper; heat through. Garnish with chives, if desired. Serves 4.

Microwave directions: In a 2-quart nonmetal casserole micro-cook celery and leek in butter or margarine, covered, on 100% power (HIGH) about 3 minutes or till tender. Stir in flour (see photo 2, page 59). Add broth and milk (see photo 3, page 59). Cook, uncovered, 4 minutes; stir. Cook, uncovered, 6 to 7 minutes more or till slightly thickened and bubbly (see photo 4, page 59). Stir after each minute. Stir in chicken or turkey, wine or broth, and pepper. Cook, covered, 1 minute more or till heated through.

Cordon Bleu Casserole

3 ounces wide noodles (2¼ cups)
3 tablespoons butter *or* margarine
3 tablespoons all-purpose flour
2 cups milk
1 cup shredded Swiss cheese (4 ounces)
¼ cup snipped parsley
1 cup chopped cooked chicken *or* frozen diced cooked chicken, thawed
½ cup diced fully cooked ham
1 4-ounce can mushroom stems and pieces, drained

Cook noodles according to the package directions. Drain (see photo 1, page 58). Place in an 8x8x2-inch baking dish.

For sauce, in a medium saucepan melt butter or margarine. Stir in flour (see photo 2, page 59). Add milk (see photo 3, page 59). Cook and stir till thickened and bubbly (see photo 4, page 59). Remove from heat. Stir in ½ cup of the cheese till melted. Stir in parsley.

Stir ½ cup of the sauce into the noodles in the baking dish. Add chicken, ham, and mushrooms to remaining sauce. Pour over noodles. Top with remaining cheese. Bake, uncovered, in a 350° oven 25 to 30 minutes or till heated through. Makes 4 servings.

Microwave Directions: On the *range top* cook noodles according to the package directions. Drain (see photo 1, page 58). Place in a nonmetal 8x8x2-inch baking dish.

Meanwhile, prepare sauce in the *microwave oven.* In a 1½-quart casserole micro-cook butter or margarine, uncovered, on 100% power (HIGH) 30 to 40 seconds or till melted. Stir in flour (see photo 2, page 59). Stir in milk (see photo 3, page 59). Cook, uncovered, 6 to 7 minutes or till thickened and bubbly (see photo 4, page 59). Stir after each minute. Stir in ½ cup of the cheese till melted. Stir in parsley.

Stir ½ *cup* of the sauce into the noodles in the baking dish. Add chicken, ham, and mushrooms to remaining sauce. Pour over noodles. Cook, covered, 6 to 7 minutes or till heated through; give the dish a half-turn once during cooking. Sprinkle remaining cheese atop.

Spanish Rice and Chicken Skillet

1⅓ cups water
⅔ cup long grain rice
1 4-ounce can chopped green chili peppers, drained
1½ teaspoons chili powder
¼ teaspoon garlic powder
2 cups chopped cooked chicken *or* frozen diced cooked chicken, thawed
1 tablespoon butter *or* margarine
1 tablespoon all-purpose flour
¾ cup milk
1 cup shredded sharp cheddar cheese
¼ cup dairy sour cream
1 small tomato, peeled, seeded, and chopped
¼ cup sliced green onion

In a 10-inch skillet combine water, uncooked rice, chili peppers, chili powder, garlic powder, ¼ teaspoon *salt*, and ⅛ teaspoon *pepper.* Bring to boiling. Reduce heat; cover and simmer 15 minutes. Stir in chicken. Cover; simmer about 5 minutes more or till rice is tender.

Meanwhile for sauce, in a small saucepan melt butter or margarine. Stir in flour (see photo 2, page 59). Add milk (see photo 3, page 59). Cook and stir till thickened and bubbly, then cook and stir 1 minute more (see photo 4, page 59). Stir sauce into rice mixture. Top with cheese; dollop sour cream on top. Sprinkle tomatoes and green onion over top. Serves 4.

Cheesy Chicken Macaroni Casserole

Try half of a 3-ounce can of French-fried onions as a crunchy alternative to the bread-crumb-almond topper.

½ cup elbow macaroni
1 10-ounce package frozen peas and carrots
2 tablespoons butter *or* margarine
2 tablespoons all-purpose flour
½ teaspoon dried basil, crushed
1⅓ cups milk
1½ cups shredded American cheese (6 ounces)
1½ cups chopped cooked chicken *or* turkey, *or* frozen diced cooked chicken, thawed
¾ cup soft bread crumbs (1 slice)
¼ cup chopped almonds
1 tablespoon butter *or* margarine, melted

Cook macaroni according to the package directions. Drain (see photo 1, page 58).

Meanwhile, place frozen peas and carrots in a colander. Rinse with running water to separate. Set aside.

In a large saucepan melt 2 tablespoons butter or margarine. Stir in flour and basil (see photo 2, page 59). Add milk (see photo 3, page 59). Cook and stir till thickened and bubbly (see photo 4, page 59). Remove from heat.

Stir in cheese till melted. Stir in macaroni, peas and carrots, and chicken or turkey. Turn mixture into a 1½-quart casserole.

Combine bread crumbs, almonds, and 1 tablespoon melted butter or margarine, then sprinkle over the casserole. Bake, uncovered, in a 350° oven 30 to 35 minutes or till heated through. Makes 6 servings.

Turkey a la King

To make Chicken a la King, simply substitute chopped cooked chicken for the turkey.

1 10-ounce package frozen peas
3 tablespoons butter *or* margarine
3 tablespoons all-purpose flour
½ teaspoon onion salt
2 cups milk
2 cups chopped cooked turkey
1 2½-ounce jar sliced mushrooms, drained
2 tablespoons chopped pimiento
1 tablespoon lemon juice
1 tablespoon dry sherry
Baked patty shells *or* toast points

Place peas in a colander. Rinse with running water to separate. Set aside.

In a medium saucepan melt butter or margarine. Stir in flour and onion salt (see photo 2, page 59). Add milk (see photo 3, page 59). Cook and stir until thickened and bubbly, then cook and stir 1 minute more (see photo 4, page 59). Stir in peas, turkey or chicken, mushrooms, pimiento, lemon juice, and sherry; heat through. Spoon into baked patty shells or over toast points. Makes 6 servings.

Microwave directions: Place peas in a colander. Rinse with running water to separate.

In a nonmetal 2-quart casserole micro-cook butter or margarine, uncovered, on 100% power (HIGH) 30 to 40 seconds or till melted. Stir in flour and onion salt (see photo 2, page 59). Stir in milk (see photo 3, page 59). Cook, uncovered, 5 to 6 minutes or till thickened and bubbly (see photo 4, page 59). Stir after each minute. Stir in peas, turkey or chicken, mushrooms, pimiento, lemon juice, and sherry. Cook mixture, covered, 3 to 4 minutes or till heated through; stir once during cooking. Spoon into baked patty shells or over toast points.

Best of the Braises

For a dish that's the best of two worlds—packed with flavor and easy to make— try braised poultry.

Begin by browning chicken or pheasant to seal in every bit of juicy flavor. Then add liquid, cover, and simmer to finish the cooking. You've just created a scrumptious dinner—with practically no effort!

Style Chicken Braise

Paella-Style Chicken Braise

We borrowed the marvelous spice saffron from Spain's traditional paella. It gives the dish a rich golden color and a wonderfully distinctive flavor.

4 *each* chicken wings *and* drumsticks
     (1½ pounds total)
2 tablespoons cooking oil *or* shortening
6 ounces chorizo links *or* Italian
     sausage links, sliced
1 large onion, cut into wedges
1 small sweet red *or* green pepper,
     cut into squares
2 cloves garlic, minced
⅛ teaspoon thread saffron
2 cups hot water
¾ cup long grain rice
2 teaspoons instant chicken bouillon
     granules
½ teaspoon turmeric
¼ teaspoon ground cumin
1 10-ounce package frozen peas
¼ cup halved pitted ripe olives
8 cherry tomatoes, halved, *or* 1 medium
     tomato, cut into 8 wedges

Rinse chicken, then pat dry. Season with salt and pepper. In a 12-inch skillet or 4-quart Dutch oven cook chicken in hot oil or shortening, uncovered, over medium heat 10 to 15 minutes or till light brown, turning to brown evenly (see photo 1). Remove chicken, reserving fat.

Cook sausage, onion, red or green pepper, and garlic in reserved fat over medium-low heat about 10 minutes or till sausage is done. Drain off fat (see photo 2). Crush saffron (see photo 3). Add saffron, water, uncooked rice, bouillon granules, turmeric, and cumin to skillet. Bring to boiling, scraping up browned bits. Place chicken on top. Reduce heat, then cover and simmer about 20 minutes or till chicken is nearly done. Turn chicken once during cooking.

Rinse peas (see photo 4). Add peas and olives to chicken mixture. Cover; cook 5 minutes more or till chicken and rice are tender (see photo 5, page 35). Gently stir in tomatoes. Serves 4.

1 Cook the chicken pieces in hot oil, turning to brown evenly, as shown. If the chicken does not have a flour-type coating on it, it will not turn a crispy golden brown. Instead, some of the skin will turn golden yellow or light brown. The meat changes from pink to white as it cooks.

2 Drain the fat from the skillet by pushing the mixture to one side. (For chicken, stack a few pieces on top of each other to one side of the skillet.) Tilt the skillet slightly, allowing the fat to pool. Use a large metal spoon to carefully transfer the hot fat to a heat-proof dish.

3 Saffron, one of the most expensive spices, comes in thin rods that look like threads. Fortunately, a little goes a long way. To release saffron's wonderful flavor, crush it by rubbing the threads between your fingers.

4 Place the frozen peas in a colander. Rinse under warm running water to thaw and separate the peas.

Chicken Cacciatore

Garden-fresh herbs work wonderfully here, too. Use three times the dried amount and omit crushing.

1 **2½- to 3-pound broiler-fryer chicken, cut up (see pages 120-121)**
2 **tablespoons olive oil *or* cooking oil**
1 **medium onion, sliced and separated into rings**
1 **clove garlic, minced**
½ **teaspoon dried rosemary**
½ **teaspoon dried thyme**
¼ **teaspoon dried oregano**
1 **7½-ounce can tomatoes, cut up**
1 **6-ounce can tomato paste**
¾ **cup dry white wine**
1 **4-ounce can mushroom stems and pieces, drained**
2 **tablespoons snipped parsley**
1 **teaspoon sugar**
  Hot cooked pasta

Rinse chicken, then pat dry. In a 12-inch skillet cook chicken in hot oil, uncovered, over medium heat 10 to 15 minutes or till light brown, turning to brown evenly (see photo 1, page 66). Add onion and garlic the last 5 minutes of cooking. Drain (see photo 2, page 66).

Crush dried rosemary, thyme, and oregano (see photo 3, page 67). In a medium bowl combine crushed herbs, *undrained* tomatoes, tomato paste, wine, mushrooms, parsley, sugar, ½ teaspoon *salt,* and ⅛ teaspoon *pepper.* Pour over chicken in skillet. Bring to boiling. Reduce heat; cover and simmer 35 to 40 minutes or till tender (see photo 5, page 35). Turn once during cooking. Serve over hot cooked pasta. Serves 6.

Oven Chicken Cacciatore: Prepare Chicken Cacciatore as above, *except* cook chicken in a 12-inch ovenproof skillet. Pour tomato mixture over and transfer skillet to a 375° oven. (*Or,* remove chicken, onion, and garlic from skillet and place, skin side up, in an ungreased 13x9x2-inch baking pan; pour tomato mixture over). Bake, covered, in a 375° oven 35 to 45 minutes or till tender (see photo 5, page 35).

Barbecued Pineapple Chicken

Want to try the oven version, but don't own an oven-proof skillet? To adapt your regular skillet, refer to the tip box on page 43.

¼ **cup all-purpose flour**
½ **teaspoon salt**
1 **2½- to 3-pound broiler-fryer chicken, cut up (see pages 120-121)**
2 **tablespoons cooking oil**
1 **8¼-ounce can crushed pineapple**
½ **cup bottled barbecue sauce**
⅓ **cup chopped green pepper**
1 **tablespoon cornstarch**
½ **teaspoon dry mustard**
  Chow mein noodles (optional)

In a plastic or paper bag combine flour and salt. Rinse chicken, then pat dry. Add chicken, 2 or 3 pieces at a time, to the bag, then shake to coat (see photo 1, page 40).

In a 12-inch skillet cook chicken in hot oil, uncovered, over medium heat 10 to 15 minutes or till golden brown, turning to brown evenly (see photo 1, page 66). Drain (see photo 2, page 66).

Meanwhile, in a small mixing bowl combine *undrained* pineapple, barbecue sauce, green pepper, cornstarch, and mustard. Pour over chicken in skillet. Bring to boiling. Reduce heat, then cover and simmer 35 to 40 minutes or till chicken is tender enough to be easily pierced with a fork (see photo 5, page 35). Turn chicken once during cooking. Serve with chow mein noodles, if desired. Makes 6 servings.

Barbecued Pineapple Chicken Bake: Prepare Barbecued Pineapple Chicken as above, *except* cook chicken in a 12-inch ovenproof skillet. Pour pineapple mixture over chicken and transfer skillet to a 375° oven. (*Or,* remove chicken from skillet and place, skin side up, in an ungreased 13x9x2-inch baking pan. Pour pineapple mixture over.) Bake, covered, in a 375° oven 35 to 45 minutes or till chicken is tender (see photo 5, page 35).

Chicken in Red Wine Sauce

A spin-off of the famous French coq au vin, this dish takes on a grey-beige color from the wine.

1 slice bacon
1 tablespoon cooking oil
1 2½- to 3-pound broiler-fryer chicken, cut up (see pages 120-121)
½ teaspoon dried marjoram
½ teaspoon dried thyme
1 cup dry red wine
1 tablespoon cognac *or* brandy
⅛ teaspoon pepper
2 bay leaves
12 pearl onions, peeled, *or* ½ of a 20-ounce package (2½ cups) frozen small whole onions, thawed
2 medium carrots, cut into 1-inch pieces
2 tablespoons cold water
1 tablespoon all-purpose flour

In a 12-inch skillet cook bacon till crisp. Remove from skillet and crumble, reserving drippings. Add oil to skillet. Rinse chicken; pat dry. Cook chicken in hot oil and drippings, uncovered, over medium heat 10 to 15 minutes or till light brown, turning to brown evenly (see photo 1, page 66). Remove chicken, reserving drippings.

Crush marjoram and thyme (see photo 3, page 67). Carefully add crushed herbs, wine, cognac or brandy, pepper, and bay leaves to skillet. Bring to boiling, scraping up browned bits. Carefully add bacon, chicken, onions, and carrots. Spoon juices over chicken. Reduce heat, then cover and simmer 35 to 40 minutes or till chicken is tender (see photo 5, page 35). Turn chicken once during cooking.

Use a slotted spoon to transfer chicken and vegetables to a heated serving platter. Cover to keep warm. Discard bay leaves. Skim fat from pan juices. Combine water and flour. Add to skillet. Cook and stir till thickened and bubbly, then cook and stir 1 minute more. Spoon sauce over chicken and vegetables. If desired, garnish with parsley sprigs. Makes 6 servings.

Easy Curry-Apple Chicken

Simple, but oh so tasty, thanks to canned apple pie filling, raisins, and peanuts.

3 pounds meaty chicken pieces (breasts, thighs, and drumsticks)
2 tablespoons cooking oil *or* shortening
1 21-ounce can apple pie filling
¼ cup raisins
2 tablespoons lemon juice
1 tablespoon curry powder
3 cups hot cooked rice
1 tablespoon cold water
1 teaspoon cornstarch
¼ cup peanuts

Rinse chicken, then pat dry. In a 12-inch skillet cook chicken in hot oil or shortening, uncovered, over medium heat 10 to 15 minutes or till light brown, turning to brown evenly (see photo 1, page 66). Drain (see photo 2, page 66).

Meanwhile, in a medium mixing bowl combine pie filling, raisins, lemon juice, and curry powder. Pour over chicken in skillet. Bring to boiling. Reduce heat, then cover and simmer 35 to 40 minutes or till chicken is tender enough to be easily pierced with a fork (see photo 5, page 35). Turn chicken once during cooking.

Arrange rice on a heated serving platter. Use a slotted spoon to transfer chicken to platter. Cover to keep warm. Use a metal spoon to skim off fat that rises to the top of the pan juices. Combine water and cornstarch. Add to apple mixture in skillet. Cook and stir till thickened and bubbly, then cook and stir 2 minutes more. Pour sauce over chicken and rice. Sprinkle with peanuts. Makes 6 servings.

Easy Curry-Apple Pheasant: Prepare Easy Curry-Apple Chicken as above, *except* substitute one 3-pound *domestic pheasant,* cut up, for the chicken pieces.

Saucy Fricassees

Braise a chicken. Then make a creamy sauce out of the cooking liquid. And what do you have? A fricassee!

Our hearty country-style fricassees start with the freshest of ingredients—homegrown if you like. Just add pure cream to create some of the richest, smoothest sauces around and you'll just know these are the most delectable dishes you've ever tasted.

Lemon-Tarragon Chicken Fricassee

Lemon-Tarragon Chicken Fricassee

1   2½- to 3-pound broiler-fryer chicken, cut up (see pages 120-121)
2   tablespoons cooking oil *or* shortening
3   stalks celery
1   large onion, chopped (1 cup)
2   teaspoons instant chicken bouillon granules
1   teaspoon dried tarragon, crushed
½   teaspoon finely shredded lemon peel
¼   teaspoon pepper
1   bay leaf
1   tablespoon butter *or* margarine
1   tablespoon all-purpose flour
⅓   cup light cream *or* milk
2   egg yolks
¼   cup snipped parsley
1   tablespoon lemon juice

Rinse chicken, then pat dry. In a 12-inch skillet cook chicken in hot oil or shortening, uncovered, over medium heat 10 to 15 minutes or till light brown, turning to brown evenly. Remove chicken, then drain off all but 2 tablespoons fat.

Bias-slice celery (see photo 1). Add celery and onion to skillet. Cook and stir 2 minutes. Carefully add bouillon granules, tarragon, lemon peel, pepper, bay leaf, and 1 cup *water*. Bring to boiling, scraping up browned bits. Add chicken. Reduce heat, then cover and simmer 35 to 40 minutes or till chicken is tender (see photo 5, page 35). Turn chicken once during cooking.

Transfer chicken and vegetables to a warm platter; cover to keep warm (see photo 2). Discard bay leaf. Skim fat from pan juices. Measure and reserve ¾ cup juices (see photo 3). In the same skillet melt butter or margarine. Stir in flour. Add reserved juices and light cream or milk all at once. Cook and stir until thickened and bubbly, then cook and stir 1 minute more.

In a small mixing bowl beat egg yolks. Gradually stir in thickened cream mixture (see photo 4). Return all to skillet. Cook and stir 1 minute. Stir in parsley and lemon juice. Pour some sauce over chicken; pass remaining. Makes 6 servings.

1 To bias-slice celery, hold a knife at a slight angle to the cutting surface and slice across the celery stalks, making ¼-inch slices.

2 Use a slotted spoon to remove the chicken pieces and vegetables from the cooking liquid, as shown. Arrange them on a warm serving platter and cover with foil to keep warm.

Spirited Chicken Fricassee

¼ cup all-purpose flour
1 teaspoon paprika
1 2½- to 3-pound broiler-fryer chicken,
   cut up (see pages 120-121)
2 tablespoons cooking oil *or* shortening
1 cup halved fresh mushrooms
⅓ cup chopped sweet red *or* green pepper
½ cup dry white wine *or* champagne
½ cup chicken broth
¼ teaspoon ground sage
1 tablespoon butter *or* margarine
1 tablespoon all-purpose flour
⅓ cup whipping cream *or* light cream
2 egg yolks

3 Pour the juices into a measuring cup. If the juices measure more than the amount indicated in the recipe, discard the excess. *Or,* if necessary, add water until the juices measure the amount the recipe indicates.

In a plastic or paper bag combine ¼ cup flour, paprika, ½ teaspoon *salt,* and ¼ teaspoon *pepper.* Rinse chicken, then pat dry. Add chicken, 2 or 3 pieces at a time, to the bag, then shake to coat (see photo 1, page 40).

In a 12-inch skillet cook chicken in hot oil, uncovered, over medium heat 10 to 15 minutes or till golden, turning to brown evenly. Remove chicken, then drain off all but 2 tablespoons fat.

Add mushrooms and red or green pepper to skillet. Cook and stir 2 minutes. Carefully add wine or champagne, chicken broth, and sage. Bring to boiling, scraping up browned bits. Add chicken. Reduce heat, then cover and simmer 35 to 40 minutes or till chicken is tender (see photo 5, page 35). Turn once during cooking.

4 In a small mixing bowl beat the egg yolks with a wire whisk. Gradually stir the thickened cream mixture into the egg yolks, as shown. Adding the hot mixture gradually to the egg yolks and constantly stirring helps prevent curdling.

Transfer chicken and vegetables to a platter; cover to keep warm (see photo 2). Skim fat from pan juices. Measure and reserve 1 cup juices (see photo 3). In the same skillet melt butter or margarine. Stir in 1 tablespoon flour. Add reserved juices and whipping or light cream all at once. Cook and stir until thickened and bubbly, then cook and stir 1 minute more.

In a small mixing bowl beat egg yolks. Gradually add thickened mixture (see photo 4). Return all to skillet. Cook and stir 1 minute. Pour some sauce over chicken; pass remaining. Serves 6.

Sautéing-In Flavor

Tender, juicy, and 100 percent pure white meat. Sound good? Then so will these recipes.

We've cooked prime boneless chicken breasts quickly over high heat, sealing in every drop of the flavorful juices. What's more, you'll save time. Each boneless chicken piece cooks in minutes.

Chicken and Vegetable Platter

Chicken and Vegetable Platter

2 whole medium chicken breasts (1½ pounds total)
1 beaten egg
2 tablespoons water
½ cup crushed shredded wheat wafers (about 10 wafers)
¼ teaspoon seasoned salt
¼ teaspoon paprika
2 tablespoons cooking oil *or* shortening
1 pound zucchini *and* crookneck squash, cut into strips (3 cups)
2 tablespoons chopped green pepper
2 tablespoons butter *or* margarine
1 medium tomato, seeded and chopped
⅛ teaspoon salt

Microwave directions: (See tip box, page 60). Prepare chicken as at left, *except* omit oil. Place chicken on a microwave baking rack in a 12x7½x2-inch nonmetal baking dish; arrange thickest portions toward outside of dish. Micro-cook, uncovered, on 100% power (HIGH) for 6 to 9 minutes or till tender. Turn dish a half-turn after 4 minutes. Cover and keep warm.

In a 1½-quart casserole combine squash, green pepper, and 2 tablespoons *water*. Cover; cook for 4 to 6 minutes or till just tender. Stir in tomato. Cover; cook for 30 seconds. Drain. Gently stir in butter and salt. Serve as at left.

Skin chicken breasts (see photo 1). Discard skin. Use a knife to cut meat away from 1 side of the breastbone (see photo 2). Scrape meat away from rib bones on 1 side (see photo 3). Repeat on other side of breast. Repeat with remaining breast; discard bones. Remove tendon from each breast half (see photo 4). Rinse chicken, then pat dry.

Combine egg and water. In shallow bowl or pie plate combine wafers, seasoned salt, and paprika. Dip chicken into egg mixture, then roll in crumb mixture, patting to coat chicken well.

In a 10-inch skillet cook chicken in hot oil or shortening over medium-high heat for 8 to 10 minutes or till tender (see photo 5, page 35). Turn occasionally to brown evenly.

Meanwhile, in a large saucepan cook squash and green pepper in hot butter or margarine 6 minutes or till squash is tender. Stir in tomato and salt; heat through. Arrange the vegetables on a warm serving platter (see photo 5). Place the chicken atop the vegetables. Serves 4.

1 Place the chicken breast on a cutting board, skin side up. To skin, use your hand to pull the skin away from the meat. Discard the skin. Repeat with re-maining chicken breast.

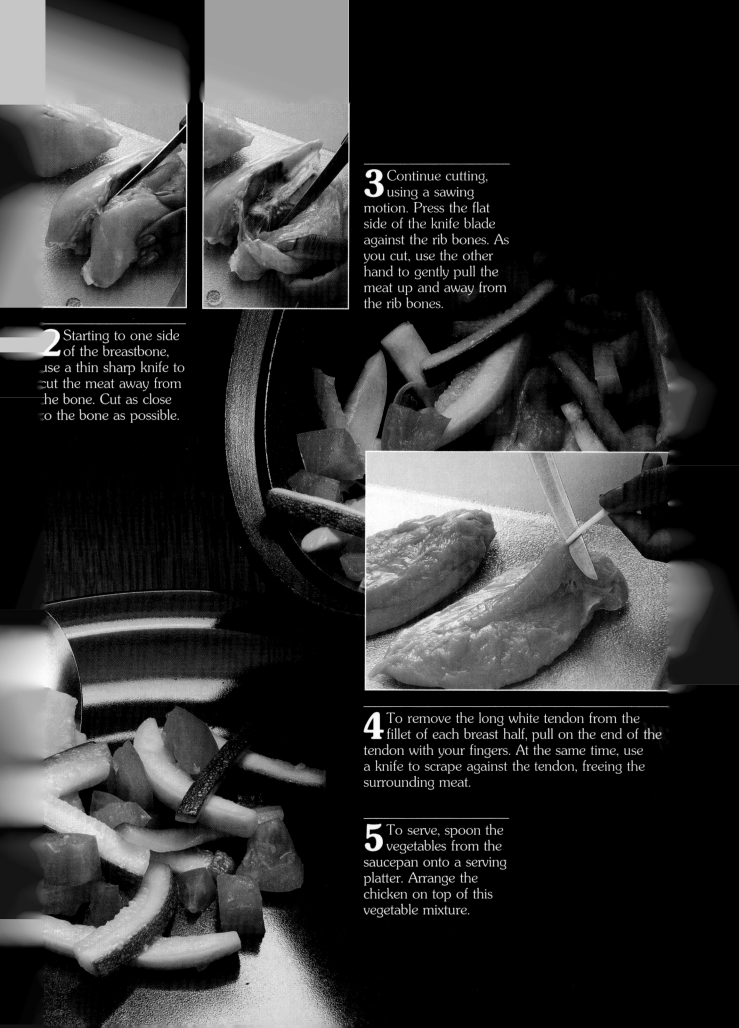

3 Continue cutting, using a sawing motion. Press the flat side of the knife blade against the rib bones. As you cut, use the other hand to gently pull the meat up and away from the rib bones.

2 Starting to one side of the breastbone, use a thin sharp knife to cut the meat away from the bone. Cut as close to the bone as possible.

4 To remove the long white tendon from the fillet of each breast half, pull on the end of the tendon with your fingers. At the same time, use a knife to scrape against the tendon, freeing the surrounding meat.

5 To serve, spoon the vegetables from the saucepan onto a serving platter. Arrange the chicken on top of this vegetable mixture.

Mushroom-Wine-Sauced Chicken Breasts

Start with a package of instant soup mix, add a little wine for a mellow flavor and some nuts for crunch, and you've got an easy, great-tasting sauce.

2 whole medium chicken breasts
    (1½ pounds total)
2 tablespoons butter *or* margarine
1 cup sliced fresh mushrooms *or* one
    4½-ounce jar sliced mushrooms,
    drained
2 tablespoons sliced almonds
⅓ cup dry white wine
⅓ cup water
1 single-serving envelope *instant* cream
    of chicken soup mix

Skin chicken breasts (see photo 1, page 76). Discard skin. Use a knife to cut meat away from 1 side of breastbone (see photo 2, page 77). Scrape meat away from rib bones on 1 side (see photo 3, page 77). Repeat on other side of breast. Repeat with remaining breast; discard bones. Remove tendon from each breast half (see photo 4, page 77). Rinse chicken; pat dry.

In a 10-inch skillet cook chicken in hot butter or margarine over medium-high heat for 5 minutes, turning occasionally to brown evenly. Add mushrooms and almonds. Cook 3 to 5 minutes more or till chicken is tender (see photo 5, page 35). Stir occasionally. Transfer chicken to a warm serving platter. Cover to keep warm.

For sauce, in a small mixing bowl stir together wine, water, and soup mix. Add to skillet. Cook and stir till thickened and bubbly, scraping up browned bits. Spoon some sauce over chicken. Pass remaining sauce. Makes 4 servings.

Lemon-Dill Chicken Breasts

Try serving this tangy chicken with hot buttered broccoli or asparagus spears.

2 whole medium chicken breasts
    (1½ pounds total)
1 tablespoon butter *or* margarine
1½ teaspoons snipped fresh dill
    or ½ teaspoon dried dillweed
¼ teaspoon pepper
1 tablespoon lemon juice

Skin chicken breasts (see photo 1, page 76). Discard skin. Use a knife to cut meat away from 1 side of breastbone (see photo 2, page 77). Scrape meat away from rib bones on 1 side (see photo 3, page 77). Repeat on other side of breast. Repeat with remaining breast; discard bones. Remove tendon from each breast half (see photo 4, page 77). Rinse chicken; pat dry.

In a 10-inch skillet melt butter or margarine. Stir in dillweed and pepper. Add chicken and cook over medium-high heat for 8 to 10 minutes or until chicken is tender (see photo 5, page 35). Turn occasionally to brown evenly.

Transfer chicken to a warm serving platter. Cover to keep warm. Reduce heat, then carefully add lemon juice to skillet. Heat and stir, scraping up browned bits. Spoon over chicken breasts. Makes 4 servings.

Cabbage-Apple Chicken Burritos

2 **whole medium chicken breasts**
   (1½ pounds total)
2 **tablespoons butter *or* margarine**
2 **cups finely shredded cabbage**
2 **medium apples, finely chopped**
⅓ **cup sliced green onion**
½ **cup dairy sour cream**
4 **teaspoons all-purpose flour**
½ **teaspoon instant chicken bouillon**
   granules
⅛ **teaspoon ground cinnamon**
6 **8- to 10-inch flour tortillas**
1 **cup shredded cheddar cheese**
   (4 ounces)
2 **tablespoons sliced green onion**

Skin chicken breasts (see photo 1, page 76). Discard skin. Use a knife to cut meat away from 1 side of the breastbone (see photo 2, page 77). Scrape meat away from rib bones on 1 side (see photo 3, page 77). Repeat on other side of breast. Repeat with remaining breast; discard bones. Remove tendon from each breast half (see photo 4, page 77). Rinse chicken, then pat dry. Cut chicken into thin bite-size strips.

In a 10-inch skillet cook and stir *half* of the chicken in hot butter or margarine over high heat 2 to 3 minutes or till tender (see photo 5, page 35). Remove chicken. Repeat with remaining chicken. Remove, reserving drippings. Add cabbage, apple, and ⅓ cup green onion to skillet. Cook till tender. Return chicken to skillet. Stir together sour cream and flour. Add to skillet along with bouillon granules, cinnamon, and ½ cup *water*. Cook and stir till bubbly.

Spoon mixture, just below center, onto 6 tortillas. Fold edge nearest filling up and over filling just till mixture is covered. Fold in 2 sides envelope fashion; roll up. Place, seam side down, in a 13x9x2-inch baking dish. Bake, covered, in a 350° oven 15 to 20 minutes or till heated through. Sprinkle cheese and 2 tablespoons green onion on top. Bake, uncovered, 2 to 3 minutes more or till cheese melts. Serves 6.

Orange Oriental Chicken

When time is at a premium, use purchased boneless chicken breasts instead of boning your own.

2 **whole medium chicken breasts**
   (1½ pounds total)
2 **tablespoons cooking oil *or* shortening**
1 **8-ounce can sliced water chestnuts,**
   drained
1 **6-ounce package frozen pea pods**
½ **teaspoon finely shredded orange peel**
½ **cup orange juice**
2 **tablespoons soy sauce**
1 **tablespoon cold water**
2 **teaspoons cornstarch**
   Hot cooked rice

Skin chicken breasts (see photo 1, page 76). Discard skin. Use a knife to cut meat away from 1 side of breastbone (see photo 2, page 77). Scrape meat away from rib bones on 1 side (see photo 3, page 77). Repeat on other side of breast. Repeat with remaining breast; discard bones. Remove tendon from each breast half (see photo 4, page 77). Rinse chicken; pat dry.

In a 10-inch skillet cook chicken in hot oil or shortening over medium-high heat for 8 minutes, turning to brown evenly. Add water chestnuts and pea pods. Cover and simmer for 2 to 3 minutes longer or till chicken is tender (see photo 5, page 35). Transfer chicken and vegetables to a warm serving platter. Cover to keep warm.

Stir together orange peel, orange juice, soy sauce, water, and cornstarch. Add to skillet, mixing well. Cook and stir till thickened and bubbly, scraping up browned bits. Cook and stir 2 minutes more. Spoon sauce over chicken and vegetables. Serve with hot cooked rice. Serves 4.

Matchless Medaillions

Just like the thrill of winning an Olympic medal, you'll win record-breaking compliments when you serve these scrumptious poultry dishes.

Each recipe begins with boneless poultry breasts pounded thin into a medaillion shape and sautéed to a golden brown. Their individual flavors, inspired by some of Italy's favorite dishes, are a reward in themselves. Come enjoy the marvelous taste of these matchless medaillions!

Turkey Parmigiana

Turkey Parmigiana

1	**medium onion, chopped (½ cup)**
1	**clove garlic, minced**
1	**tablespoon cooking oil**
1	**16-ounce can tomatoes, cut up**
1	**8-ounce can tomato sauce**
1	**teaspoon dried basil**
1	**teaspoon dried oregano**
¼	**teaspoon dried thyme**
1	**bay leaf**
4	**turkey breast tenderloin steaks (1 pound total)**
¼	**cup all-purpose flour**
1	**beaten egg**
¾	**cup fine dry bread crumbs**
2	**to 4 tablespoons cooking oil**
4	**slices mozzarella cheese (6 ounces)**
½	**cup grated Parmesan cheese**

For sauce, in a medium saucepan cook onion and garlic in 1 tablespoon hot oil. Add tomatoes and tomato sauce. Crush basil, oregano, and thyme (see photo 1). Add to saucepan along with bay leaf. Bring to boiling. Reduce heat, then cover and simmer 10 minutes. Uncover, then simmer 5 minutes more. Discard bay leaf.

Meanwhile, rinse turkey; pat dry. Place 1 steak between 2 pieces of clear plastic wrap, then pound to ¼-inch thickness (see photo 2). Repeat. In a plastic bag combine flour, ¼ teaspoon *salt,* and ⅛ teaspoon *pepper.* Add 1 steak, then shake to coat. Shake off excess flour. Repeat. In a pie plate combine egg and 2 tablespoons *water.* Place bread crumbs in another pie plate. Dip steaks into egg mixture, then coat with bread crumbs (see photo 3).

In a 10-inch skillet cook 2 steaks in 2 tablespoons hot oil over medium heat about 3 minutes on each side or till golden brown. Remove steaks. Repeat, adding more oil if necessary.

Place 2 steaks in a 12x7½x2-inch baking dish. Top with *half* of the tomato sauce and *half* of the mozzarella and Parmesan cheese. Repeat layers. Bake, uncovered, in a 400° oven 15 to 20 minutes or till heated through. Serves 6.

1 Place the dried herbs in the bottom of a mortar or small bowl. Use a pestle or the back of a spoon to crush. Crushing dried herbs like this helps release the most flavor.

2 Place one turkey tenderloin steak between two pieces of clear plastic wrap. Working from the center to the edges, pound the steak lightly with the flat side of a meat mallet, as shown. Pound until the steak measures ¼ inch thick with a ruler. Remove the plastic wrap from the steak and repeat with the remaining turkey steaks.

3 Dip one turkey steak into egg mixture. Then coat with the bread crumbs, patting to cover the steak well. Repeat with the remaining turkey steaks. Keep the wet and dry mixtures separate by using one hand for the egg mixture and the other hand for the bread crumbs.

Chicken with Marsala

2 **whole medium chicken breasts (1½ pounds total), skinned, boned, and halved lengthwise (see page 76)**
¼ **cup all-purpose flour**
⅛ **teaspoon pepper**
2 **tablespoons butter *or* margarine**
2 **tablespoons sliced green onion**
¼ **cup chicken broth**
¼ **cup dry Marsala**
2 **tablespoons snipped parsley**

Rinse chicken; pat dry. Place 1 chicken breast half between 2 pieces of clear plastic wrap, then pound to ⅛-inch thickness (see photo 2). Repeat with remaining chicken. In a pie plate combine flour and pepper. Lightly press 1 chicken piece into mixture (see photo 3). Shake off excess flour. Repeat with remaining chicken.

In a 12-inch skillet cook chicken in hot butter or margarine over medium-high heat for 4 minutes, turning to brown evenly. Add onion and cook about 1 minute or till chicken is tender and easily pierced with a fork (see photo 5, page 35). Remove from heat.

Carefully add broth and Marsala to skillet. Cook, uncovered, 2 to 3 minutes or till sauce thickens, stirring occasionally. Transfer chicken to a serving platter, then spoon sauce over. Sprinkle with parsley. Makes 4 servings.

Filled Suprêmes

Supreme indeed! These dishes featuring flattened boneless poultry breasts are superb as well as suprême. Superb describes the flavor. Suprême describes the way they're made—with a tasty surprise rolled up inside. Many of these recipes traditionally call for veal. But we have made the economical choice of substituting chicken or turkey. Even the most trained tastebuds will have a hard time detecting the difference.

Chicken Cordon Bleu

Rinse chicken, then pat dry. Place 1 chicken piece, boned side up, between 2 pieces of clear plastic wrap. Working from the center to the edges, pound lightly with a meat mallet to form a rectangle about ¼ inch thick (see photo 2, page 82). Remove the plastic wrap. Repeat with remaining chicken pieces.

Place *1* slice of prosciutto and *1* slice of cheese on *each* cutlet (see photo 1). Fold in the bottom and sides (see photo 2). Roll up jelly-roll style; secure with wooden toothpicks (see photo 3).

In a 10-inch skillet cook rolls in *3 tablespoons* hot butter or margarine over medium-low heat for 20 minutes or till tender (see photo 5, page 35). Turn to brown evenly. Remove toothpicks.

Meanwhile, for sauce, in a small saucepan melt *2 tablespoons* butter or margarine. Add mushrooms and garlic (see photo 4). Cook till tender. Stir in 1 tablespoon flour. Add milk all at once. Stir together sour cream, 1 tablespoon flour, and nutmeg. Stir into mixture in saucepan. Cook and stir till thickened and bubbly, then cook and stir 2 minutes more.

Meanwhile, cook noodles according to the package directions. Drain. Transfer noodles and chicken to a platter; top with sauce. Serves 4.

1 Place a slice of prosciutto or ham and a slice of cheese on each cutlet. Use kitchen shears to trim the meat and cheese to fit, if necessary.

2 Fold in the bottom edge and sides of *each* cutlet about ½ inch. This helps hold the meat and cheese filling inside and gives the roll a finished look.

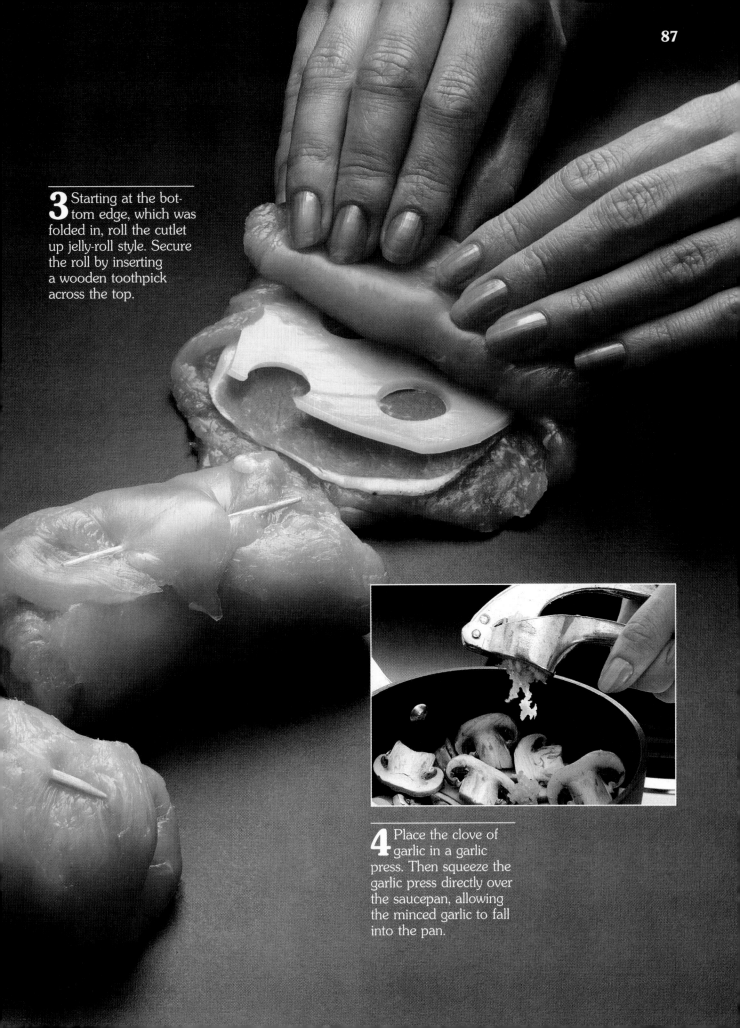

3 Starting at the bottom edge, which was folded in, roll the cutlet up jelly-roll style. Secure the roll by inserting a wooden toothpick across the top.

4 Place the clove of garlic in a garlic press. Then squeeze the garlic press directly over the saucepan, allowing the minced garlic to fall into the pan.

Turkey Florentine With Orange Sauce

The black poppy seed are a nice contrast to the brightly colored orange sauce.

4 **turkey breast tenderloin steaks (1 pound total)**
1 **16-ounce can mandarin orange sections**
½ **of a 10-ounce package frozen chopped spinach, thawed and well drained**
2 **tablespoons chopped almonds *or* macadamia nuts**
1 **tablespoon lemon juice**
1 **tablespoon butter *or* margarine, melted**
½ **teaspoon poppy seed**
2 **tablespoons sugar**
1 **tablespoon cornstarch**

Rinse turkey, then pat dry. Place 1 steak between 2 pieces of clear plastic wrap. Working from the center to the edges, pound lightly with a meat mallet to form a rectangle about ¼ inch thick (see photo 2, page 82). Remove the plastic wrap. Repeat with remaining turkey steaks. Sprinkle lightly with salt.

Drain mandarin orange sections, reserving syrup. For filling, in a small mixing bowl combine ¼ *cup* of the oranges, spinach, and almonds or macadamia nuts. Drizzle with lemon juice, then toss lightly till well mixed.

Spoon about ¼ *cup* of the filling onto the center of *each* steak (see photo 1, page 86). Roll up jelly-roll style and secure (see photo 3, page 87).

Place rolls in a 10x6x2-inch baking dish. Brush with melted butter or margarine. Sprinkle with poppy seed. Bake, covered, in a 350° oven for 30 to 35 minutes or till tender (see photo 5, page 35). Remove toothpicks.

Meanwhile, for sauce, in a medium saucepan combine sugar, cornstarch, and a dash *salt.* Add reserved syrup. Cook and stir over medium heat till thickened and bubbly, then cook and stir 2 minutes more. Stir in remaining orange sections. Spoon sauce over turkey rolls. Serves 4.

Rum-Raisin-Stuffed Chicken Breasts

Plump, rum-flavored raisins are the sweet treat tucked inside these tender, juicy chicken breasts.

½ **cup raisins**
¼ **cup water**
2 **tablespoons rum *or* ¼ teaspoon rum flavoring**
2 **whole medium chicken breasts (1½ pounds total), skinned, boned, and halved lengthwise (see page 76)**
⅓ **to ½ cup toasted wheat germ**
2 **tablespoons butter *or* margarine, melted**

For filling, in a small saucepan combine raisins, water, and rum or rum flavoring. Bring to boiling. Reduce heat; simmer, uncovered, for 5 minutes. Remove from heat; let stand 10 minutes.

Meanwhile, rinse chicken, then pat dry. Place 1 chicken piece, boned side up, between 2 pieces of clear plastic wrap. Working from the center to the edges, pound lightly with a meat mallet to form a rectangle about ¼ inch thick (see photo 2, page 82). Remove the plastic wrap. Repeat with remaining chicken pieces. Sprinkle lightly with salt, if desired.

Spoon about *2 tablespoons* of the filling onto the center of *each* cutlet (see photo 1, page 86). Fold in the bottom and sides (see photo 2, page 86). Roll up jelly-roll style and secure with wooden toothpicks (see photo 3, page 87).

Place wheat germ in a pie plate or shallow bowl. Brush rolls with melted butter or margarine. Roll in wheat germ, patting to coat well. Place rolls in a 10x6x2-inch baking dish. Bake, uncovered, in a 350° oven 20 to 25 minutes or till tender (see photo 5, page 35). Remove toothpicks. Makes 4 servings.

Chicken Kiev

¼ cup butter *or* margarine, softened
1 tablespoon finely chopped fresh chervil
    or 1 teaspoon dried chervil, crushed
1½ teaspoons snipped fresh chives *or*
    ½ teaspoon freeze-dried chives
1 clove garlic, minced
2 whole medium chicken breasts
    (1½ pounds total), skinned, boned,
    and halved lengthwise (see page 76)
3 tablespoons all-purpose flour
1 beaten egg
⅓ cup fine dry bread crumbs
    Cooking oil for deep-fat frying

In a small mixing bowl combine butter or margarine, chervil, and chives. Add garlic (see photo 4, page 87). Mix well. On waxed paper shape into four 2-inch-long sticks; chill till firm.

Rinse chicken, then pat dry. Place 1 chicken piece, boned side up, between 2 pieces of clear plastic wrap. Working from the center to the edges, pound lightly with a meat mallet to form a rectangle about ¼ inch thick (see photo 2, page 82). Remove the plastic wrap. Repeat with remaining chicken pieces.

Place *1* butter stick in the center of *each* cutlet (see photo 1, page 86). Fold in the bottom and sides (see photo 2, page 86). Roll up jelly-roll style (see photo 3, page 87). Press all edges together gently with your fingers to seal.

In a pie plate combine flour, ½ teaspoon *salt*, and ¼ teaspoon *pepper*. Coat rolls with mixture; shake off excess. In a small mixing bowl combine egg and 1 tablespoon *water*. Place bread crumbs in a pie plate. Dip 1 roll into egg mixture; roll in bread crumbs. Repeat with remaining rolls. Cover; chill 1 hour.

In a 3-quart saucepan or deep-fat fryer heat 1¼ inches oil to 375°. Carefully lower 2 rolls, 1 at a time, into hot oil (see photo 3, page 93). Fry 4 to 5 minutes or till brown. Carefully remove and drain (see photo 4, page 93). Keep warm while frying remaining rolls. Makes 4 servings.

Crab-Stuffed Chicken Rolls

2 whole medium chicken breasts
    (1½ pounds total), skinned, boned,
    and halved lengthwise (see page 76)
1 6-ounce package frozen crab meat,
    thawed and well drained
½ of an 8-ounce package frozen cut
    asparagus, thawed
2 tablespoons dry white wine
2 tablespoons butter *or* margarine, melted
½ teaspoon paprika
1 tablespoon butter *or* margarine
1 tablespoon all-purpose flour
⅔ cup milk
2 tablespoons snipped parsley
2 tablespoons dry white wine

Rinse chicken, then pat dry. Place 1 chicken piece, boned side up, between 2 pieces of clear plastic wrap. Working from the center to the edges, pound lightly with a meat mallet to form a rectangle about ¼ inch thick (see photo 2, page 82). Remove the plastic wrap. Repeat with remaining chicken pieces.

For filling, in a small mixing bowl combine *half* of the crab, asparagus, and ¼ teaspoon *pepper*. Drizzle with 2 tablespoons wine, then toss lightly till well mixed.

Spoon about ¼ *cup* of the filling onto center of *each* cutlet (see photo 1, page 86). Fold in the bottom and sides (see photo 2, page 86). Roll up jelly-roll style; secure (see photo 3, page 87).

Place rolls in a 10x6x2-inch baking dish. Brush with 2 tablespoons melted butter or margarine. Sprinkle with paprika. Bake, covered, in a 350° oven for 20 to 25 minutes or till tender (see photo 5, page 35). Remove toothpicks.

Meanwhile, for sauce, in a small saucepan melt 1 tablespoon butter or margarine. Stir in flour. Add milk all at once. Cook and stir till thickened and bubbly, then cook and stir 1 minute more. Stir in remaining crab, parsley, and 2 tablespoons wine; heat through. Spoon sauce over chicken rolls. Makes 4 servings.

Batter-Fried Chicken

Remember when Grandma used to load the table with her crispy fried chicken? Her "secret" recipe was simply the best—so good that you just couldn't help licking your fingers.

Grandma's traditions live on in these forget-me-not chicken recipes: They're batter-dipped and deep-fried to crisp perfection. In fact, they're so good, Grandma would be proud to call them her own!

Herbed Batter-Fried Chicken

Herbed Batter-Fried Chicken

1   2½- to 3-pound broiler-fryer chicken, cut up (see pages 120-121)
½   teaspoon dried thyme, crushed
1   bay leaf
¾   cup all-purpose flour
1   teaspoon baking powder
1   teaspoon dried thyme, savory, marjoram, *or* sage, crushed
1   beaten egg
⅔   cup buttermilk
¼   cup cooking oil
     Shortening *or* cooking oil for deep-fat frying

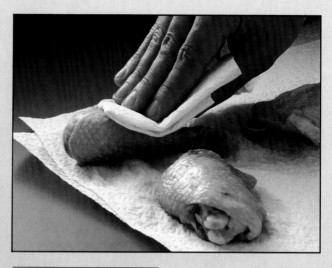

Rinse chicken. In a large saucepan combine chicken, ½ teaspoon thyme, bay leaf, and dash *salt*. Cover with water. Bring to boiling. Reduce heat, then cover and simmer for 20 minutes. Drain, then pat dry (see photo 1).

For batter, combine flour; baking powder; 1 teaspoon thyme, savory, marjoram, or sage; ½ teaspoon *salt;* and ¼ teaspoon *pepper*. Combine egg, buttermilk, and ¼ cup cooking oil. Add to dry ingredients. Beat till smooth (see photo 2).

Meanwhile, in a heavy 3-quart saucepan or deep-fat fryer heat 1¼ inches shortening or oil to 365°. Dip chicken, 1 piece at a time, into the batter. Carefully lower into the deep hot oil (see photo 3). Fry, a few pieces at a time, 2 to 3 minutes or till golden brown. Carefully remove and drain (see photo 4). Keep hot in a warm oven while frying remaining chicken. Serves 6.

1 Drain the cooked chicken and pat it dry with paper towels. This helps the batter cling to the chicken more evenly. It also removes water which, if left on, could cause the hot oil to spatter dangerously.

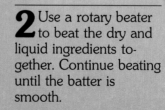

2 Use a rotary beater to beat the dry and liquid ingredients together. Continue beating until the batter is smooth.

3 Carefully lower a chicken piece into hot oil. To keep a constant temperature and prevent chicken from becoming greasy, fry only a few pieces at a time. Use a deep-fat frying thermometer to monitor temperature. (Be sure bulb doesn't touch pan.)

4 Use tongs to carefully remove the chicken pieces, as shown. Drain well on several layers of paper towels.

Chicken Tempura

For a fun participation dinner, bring the fondue cooker and ready-to-cook food to the table.

Ginger Tempura Sauce
2 **whole medium chicken breasts (1½ pounds total), skinned, boned, and halved lengthwise (see page 76)**
   Peanut oil *or* cooking oil for deep-fat frying
¾ **cup all-purpose flour**
2 **tablespoons cornstarch**
¼ **teaspoon garlic salt**
1 **egg yolk**
1 **teaspoon sesame oil**
1 **stiffly beaten egg white**
½ **pound green beans, cut into 2-inch pieces (about 2 cups)**
1 **cup halved fresh mushrooms**
1 **cup cauliflower flowerets**
1 **cup broccoli flowerets**

Prepare Ginger Tempura Sauce; set aside. Rinse chicken, then pat dry (see photo 1, page 92). Cut into 1-inch pieces.

Pour peanut or cooking oil into an electric fondue cooker to a 2-inch depth. Heat to 425° on the range top. Add 1 teaspoon *salt*. Transfer to the fondue base set on the highest setting. (*Or,* in a heavy 3-quart saucepan heat 2 inches of peanut or cooking oil to 400°.)

Meanwhile, for batter, in a large mixing bowl combine flour, cornstarch, and garlic salt. Make a well in the center. In a small mixing bowl combine yolk, sesame oil, and ¾ cup *ice water*. Add to dry ingredients. Slowly stir just till moistened. Fold in egg white. Use batter at once.

Dip chicken and vegetables, a few pieces at a time, into the batter. Carefully lower into the deep hot oil (see photo 3, page 93). Fry, a few pieces at a time, 2 to 3 minutes or till golden brown. Carefully remove and drain (see photo 4, page 93). Pass warm Ginger Tempura Sauce. Makes 4 servings.

Ginger Tempura Sauce: In a small saucepan combine ½ cup *water*, 2 tablespoons *dry sherry,* 2 tablespoons *soy sauce*, 1 teaspoon *grated gingerroot,* and ½ teaspoon *instant chicken bouillon granules.* Cook and stir till boiling. Makes ¾ cup sauce.

Beer Batter-Fried Chicken

The crisp and crunchy coating puffs up around the chicken as it fries.

1 **2½- to 3-pound broiler-fryer chicken, cut up (see pages 120-121)**
1 **cup packaged biscuit mix**
1 **teaspoon dry mustard**
½ **teaspoon salt**
¼ **teaspoon ground red pepper**
1 **beaten egg**
½ **cup beer**
   Shortening *or* cooking oil for deep-fat frying

Rinse chicken. In a large saucepan combine chicken and dash *salt*. Cover with water. Bring to boiling. Reduce heat; cover and simmer 20 minutes. Drain; pat dry (see photo 1, page 92).

For batter, in a large mixing bowl combine biscuit mix, mustard, salt, and red pepper. In a small mixing bowl combine egg and beer. Add to dry ingredients. Beat until batter is smooth (see photo 2, page 92).

Meanwhile, in a heavy 3-quart saucepan or deep-fat fryer heat 1¼ inches shortening or oil to 365°. Dip chicken, 1 piece at a time, into the batter. Carefully lower into the deep hot oil (see photo 3, page 93). Fry, a few pieces at a time, 2 to 3 minutes or till golden brown. Carefully remove and drain (see photo 4, page 93). Keep hot in a warm oven while frying remaining chicken. Makes 6 servings.

Deep-Fried Cornmeal Chicken

We fried our cornmeal batter in 350° oil so the pieces retain the golden color of the cornmeal.

1   **2½- to 3-pound broiler-fryer chicken, cut up (see pages 120-121)**
⅔   **cup all-purpose flour**
⅓   **cup yellow cornmeal**
1   **1¼-ounce envelope taco seasoning mix**
1   **teaspoon baking powder**
1   **beaten egg**
⅔   **cup milk**
2   **tablespoons cooking oil**
    Shortening *or* cooking oil for deep-fat frying

Rinse chicken. Place chicken in a large saucepan. Cover with water. Bring to boiling. Reduce heat, then cover and simmer for 20 minutes. Drain, then pat dry (see photo 1, page 92).

For batter, in a large mixing bowl combine flour, cornmeal, taco seasoning mix, and baking powder. In a small mixing bowl combine egg, milk, and 2 tablespoons oil. Add to dry ingredients. Beat until smooth (see photo 2, page 92).

Meanwhile, in a heavy 3-quart saucepan or deep-fat fryer heat 1¼ inches shortening or oil to 350°. Dip chicken, 1 piece at a time, into the batter. Carefully lower into the deep hot oil (see photo 3, page 93). Fry, a few pieces at a time, for 2 to 3 minutes or till golden brown. Carefully remove and drain (see photo 4, page 93). Keep hot in a warm oven while frying remaining chicken. Makes 6 servings.

Sesame Chicken Wings with Sweet-Sour Sauce

Makes a great bite-size appetizer at your next Oriental dinner or any party.

    Sweet-Sour Sauce
16   **chicken wings (2½ pounds total)**
½   **cup all-purpose flour**
1   **tablespoon sesame seed**
¾   **teaspoon salt**
1   **beaten egg**
½   **cup water**
    Shortening *or* cooking oil for deep-fat frying

Prepare Sweet-Sour Sauce; set aside. Rinse chicken; pat dry (see photo 1, page 92). With a sharp knife, cut off and discard wing tips, then cut wings in half at the joint.

For batter, in a large mixing bowl combine flour, sesame seed, and salt. In a small mixing bowl combine egg and water. Add to dry ingredients. Beat until smooth (see photo 2, page 92).

Meanwhile, in a heavy 3-quart saucepan or deep-fat fryer heat 1¼ inches shortening or oil to 365°. Dip chicken, 1 piece at a time, into the batter. Carefully lower into the deep hot oil (see photo 3, page 93). Fry, a few pieces at a time, about 5 minutes or till golden brown. Carefully remove and drain (see photo 4, page 93). Keep hot in a warm oven while frying remaining chicken. Serve with Sweet-Sour Sauce. Makes 32 appetizers.

Sweet-Sour Sauce: In a small saucepan stir together ⅓ cup *brown sugar* and 2 teaspoons *cornstarch*. Add ¼ cup *cider vinegar*, ¼ cup *apple juice*, 1 tablespoon *soy sauce*, and ¼ teaspoon *ground ginger*. Cook and stir until mixture is thickened and bubbly, then cook and stir 2 minutes more. Makes ¾ cup sauce.

Stew 'n' Dumplings

Burr-r-r. There's nothing like a piping hot, hearty stew to warm you through and offer real sustenance on a crisp fall evening or nippy winter day. Our simmered-in-the-pot specialties are filled with made-from-scratch dumplings or noodles. And their flavors are some of the best around. So the next time the forecast calls for a blustery day, let a hearty bowl of one of these stews chase the chills away.

Home-Style Chicken and Dumplings

Home-Style Chicken And Dumplings

1 **5- to 6-pound stewing chicken, cut up**
4 **stalks celery, sliced (2 cups)**
2 **large carrots, shredded (1 cup)**
1 **large onion, chopped (1 cup)**
1½ **teaspoons dried basil, crushed**
½ **teaspoon dried marjoram, crushed**
2 **bay leaves**
1 **cup all-purpose flour**
2 **teaspoons baking powder**
1 **beaten egg**
¼ **cup milk**
2 **tablespoons cooking oil**
½ **cup all-purpose flour**
¼ **cup snipped parsley**

In a 6-quart Dutch oven combine chicken, celery, carrots, onion, basil, marjoram, bay leaves, 1 teaspoon *salt*, and ¼ teaspoon *pepper*. Add 8 cups *water* (see photo 1). Bring to boiling. Reduce heat; cover and simmer 2 to 2½ hours or till chicken is tender (see photo 4, page 9). Remove from heat. Remove chicken. Discard bay leaves. Use a metal spoon to skim fat that rises to the surface. Reserve *half* of the chicken and broth for another use (see tip box, page 100). Return remaining chicken and broth to boiling.

For batter, in a large mixing bowl combine 1 cup flour, baking powder, and ½ teaspoon *salt*. In a small mixing bowl combine egg, milk, and oil. Add to flour mixture, stirring just till moistened (see photo 2). Drop batter from a spoon onto the chicken in the broth, making 6 dumplings (see photo 3). Return to boiling. Reduce heat; cover tightly and simmer 12 to 15 minutes or till a toothpick inserted in a dumpling comes out clean. *Do not lift cover.* Use a slotted spoon to transfer dumplings and chicken to soup plates. Keep warm.

Combine 1 cup *cold water* and ½ cup flour (see photo 4). Add to broth, mixing well. Cook and stir till thickened and bubbly, then cook and stir 1 minute more. Add parsley. Season with salt and pepper. Spoon thickened broth onto each serving. Makes 6 servings.

1 Pour the water into the pan; it should cover the ingredients so they will cook evenly. Control the heat so the liquid simmers (bubbles form slowly and burst before reaching the surface).

2 Stir the dumpling mixture with a fork *just* until the dry ingredients are moistened. The mixture should appear lumpy. Do not try to beat the mixture smooth. This would make the dumplings tough and heavy instead of light and airy.

3 Drop the dumpling dough from a spoon directly onto the chicken in the bubbling broth, as shown. Make 6 mounds. Cover tightly, then reduce heat and simmer. *Lift cover only after indicated cooking time to see if dumplings are done.* (A toothpick inserted in the center should come out clean.) Lifting the cover too early makes the dumplings fall, giving them a heavy texture.

4 Place the cold water and flour in a screw-top jar. Shake well to combine, as shown. (*Or,* simply stir cold water slowly into flour.)

Chicken and Noodles

You may want to use 5 or 6 ounces of frozen noodles instead of making the noodles from scratch.

 1   **5- to 6-pound stewing chicken *or* two 2½- to 3-pound broiler-fryer chickens, cut up (see pages 120-121)**
 4   **stalks celery with leaves, cut up**
 1   **large carrot, sliced**
 1   **large onion, cut up**
 6   **whole black peppers**
 2   **sprigs parsley**
1½   **teaspoons dried basil, oregano, *or* marjoram, crushed**
 2   **bay leaves**
      Egg Noodles
 1   **cup broccoli flowerets and thinly sliced stems *or* thinly sliced zucchini**
 ¼   **cup chopped celery**
 ¼   **cup chopped onion**
 ½   **teaspoon dried thyme, sage, basil, *or* oregano, crushed**
 2   **tablespoons all-purpose flour**

In a 5-quart Dutch oven combine chicken; 4 stalks cut-up celery; carrot; 1 large cut-up onion; peppers; parsley; 1½ teaspoons basil, oregano, or marjoram; bay leaves; and 1 teaspoon *salt.* Add 6 cups *water* (see photo 1, page 98). Bring to boiling. Reduce heat; cover and simmer 2 to 2½ hours or till chicken is tender (see photo 5, page 35). (Simmer broiler-fryer chickens for 1 hour.) Meanwhile, prepare Egg Noodles.

Remove from heat. Remove chicken. Line a sieve with several cheesecloth layers, then set sieve over a large bowl. Ladle broth through. Discard cheesecloth. Use a metal spoon to skim fat that rises to the surface. When chicken is cool, remove meat from bones and chop. Discard skin and bones. Reserve *half* of the meat (about 2½ cups) and broth (about 3 cups) for another use (see tip box at right).

Bring the remaining broth to boiling. Add noodles; broccoli or zucchini; ¼ cup chopped celery; ¼ cup chopped onion; ½ teaspoon thyme, sage, basil, or oregano; and ½ teaspoon *salt.* Cover, then reduce heat and simmer 10 to 15 minutes or till noodles are tender. Add chicken. Combine flour and ¼ cup *cold water* (see photo 4, page 99). Add to broth, mixing well. Cook and stir till thickened and bubbly, then cook and stir 1 minute more. Makes 6 servings.

Egg Noodles: In a small mixing bowl combine 1 beaten *egg,* 2 tablespoons *milk,* 1 tablespoon snipped *chives,* and ¼ teaspoon *salt.* Add enough *all-purpose flour* (no more than 1 cup) to make a stiff dough. Knead gently to blend. Cover, then let rest 10 minutes. On a well-floured surface roll dough into a 16x12-inch rectangle. Let rest 20 minutes. Roll up loosely, then cut into ¼-inch slices. Unroll, then cut into desired lengths. Spread out on a rack and let dry 2 hours. Makes about 5 ounces noodles.

Storing Stewed Chicken and Broth

When a recipe tells you to reserve some chicken and broth for later use, it's your chance to save some time later on. Simply place the chicken and broth in a covered container. Label container with the date, contents, and amount. Then store in the refrigerator for several days or in the freezer for up to six months. When you need a fast meal, use the chicken and broth to create a quick Chicken and Dumplings or Chicken and Noodles dinner.

Creamed Chicken Stew with Cornmeal Dumplings

1	2½- to 3-pound broiler-fryer chicken, cut up (see pages 120-121)
1½	teaspoons instant chicken bouillon granules
4	sprigs parsley
2	bay leaves
1½	teaspoons dried savory, crushed Cornmeal Dumplings
1	cup frozen loose-pack peas
1	cup frozen small whole onions
1	cup light cream
½	cup all-purpose flour
¼	teaspoon ground nutmeg

In a 4-quart Dutch oven combine chicken, bouillon granules, ½ teaspoon *salt*, and ½ teaspoon *pepper*. Add 4 cups *water* (see photo 1, page 98). For bouquet garni, fold a square piece of cheesecloth into several layers. Place parsley, bay leaves, and savory in center. Tie edges together, forming a bag. Add to Dutch oven. Bring to boiling. Reduce heat. Cover; simmer 1 hour. Remove from heat; discard bouquet garni. Use metal spoon to skim fat from surface. Meanwhile, prepare Cornmeal Dumplings.

Bring stew to boiling. Add peas and onions. Return to boiling. Drop dumpling batter from a spoon onto the stew, making 6 dumplings (see photo 3, page 99). Reduce heat; cover tightly and simmer 10 to 12 minutes or till dumplings are done. *Do not lift cover.* Transfer dumplings and chicken to soup plates. Keep warm.

Combine cream, flour, and nutmeg (see photo 4, page 99). Add to stew; mix well. Cook and stir till thickened and bubbly. Cook and stir 1 minute more. Season with salt and pepper. Spoon thickened broth onto each serving. Serves 6.

Cornmeal Dumplings: In a small mixing bowl combine ½ cup *all-purpose flour*, ⅓ cup *yellow cornmeal*, 1½ teaspoons *baking powder*, ¼ teaspoon *garlic salt*, and dash *pepper*. Combine 1 beaten *egg*, 2 tablespoons *milk*, and 2 tablespoons *cooking oil*. Add to flour mixture; stir just till moistened (see photo 2, page 98).

Chicken Soup With Matzo Balls

A stew with outstanding flavor and light matzo balls.

2	eggs
½	cup matzo meal
¼	cup club soda
2	tablespoons rendered chicken fat *or* shortening, melted
1	2½- to 3-pound broiler-fryer chicken, cut up (see pages 120-121)
2	stalks celery, halved
1	large yellow onion with skin, halved
6	sprigs parsley
6	whole black peppers
½	teaspoon dried dillweed
2	bay leaves
3	medium carrots, cut into ½-inch slices (1 cup)
2	medium parsnips, cut into ½-inch slices (1⅔ cups)
2	small leeks, sliced (1½ cups)

For matzo balls, beat eggs well. Add matzo meal, club soda, chicken fat or shortening, ½ teaspoon *salt*, and dash *pepper*. Mix till smooth. Cover and chill at least 2 hours.

Meanwhile, in a 4-quart Dutch oven combine chicken, celery, onion, and 1 teaspoon *salt*. Add 5 cups *water* (see photo 1, page 98). For bouquet garni, fold a square piece of cheesecloth into several layers. Place parsley, black peppers, dill, and bay leaves in center. Tie edges together, forming a bag. Add to Dutch oven. Bring to boiling. Reduce heat. Cover; simmer 1 hour.

Remove chicken from broth. Cover broth; continue simmering. When chicken is cool, remove meat from bones and chop. Discard skin and bones. Remove broth from heat; discard onion, celery, and bouquet garni. Use a metal spoon to skim fat that rises to the surface. Add chicken, carrots, parsnips, and leeks. Return to boiling.

Drop matzo batter from a spoon onto broth, making 8 mounds (see photo 3, page 99). Reduce heat; cover tightly and simmer 30 minutes. *Do not lift cover.* Makes 6 servings.

Roasted Duck and Goose

You don't have to dine out at a fancy restaurant to enjoy gourmet-style duck and goose dishes. It's simple to feast on these special occasion delicacies at home. Just follow our easy-to-use directions for roasting your own duck and goose.

We also show you how to cut up and serve a bird with Oriental finesse. Now you and your friends can savor a touch of the Orient—tonight or any night!

Roast Duck with Kumquat Sauce

Roast Duck with Kumquat Sauce

1 **4- to 5-pound domestic duckling**
3 **preserved kumquats**
⅓ **cup orange juice**
1 **tablespoon cornstarch**
1 **teaspoon instant chicken bouillon granules**
2 **tablespoons toasted chopped pecans**
1 **tablespoon orange liqueur**

Rinse duck, then pat dry. Tuck drumsticks under the band of skin across the tail. Skewer neck skin to the back. Twist wing tips under the back. Prick skin well all over (see photo 1).

Place bird, breast side up, on a rack in a shallow roasting pan. Insert a meat thermometer into thigh meat (see photo 4, page 17). Roast, uncovered, in a 375° oven for 1¾ to 2¼ hours or till meat thermometer registers 180° to 185° (see photo 4, page 9). Remove fat during roasting (see photo 2). Cover; let stand 15 minutes.

To carve with an Oriental flair, place bird, breast side up, on a carving board. With a sharp cleaver, cut in half lengthwise. Remove wings and legs (see illustration 3). Set aside.

Cut backbone off each half; cut into bite-size pieces. Reassemble on ovenproof platter. Cut each wing and leg into 2 or 3 pieces. Arrange beside backbone (see illustration 4).

Cut remaining halves in half lengthwise, then cut into small pieces. Reassemble into original shape on platter (see illustration 5). Cover and reheat in a 375° oven 10 minutes.

Meanwhile, prepare sauce. Thinly slice kumquats, removing seeds. In a small saucepan combine orange juice, cornstarch, bouillon granules, and ½ cup *water*. Cook and stir till thickened and bubbly, then cook and stir 2 minutes more. Add kumquats, nuts, and orange liqueur; heat through. If desired, garnish duck with lemon leaves and additional kumquats. Pass sauce. Makes 6 servings.

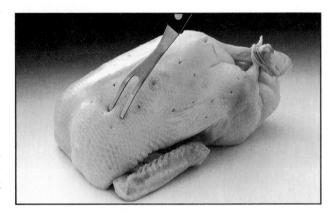

1 Using a kitchen fork, prick the skin of the bird well all over. This allows the fat to escape while the bird is roasting.

2 To prevent the fat from spattering, remove the excess fat several times during roasting. To do this, take the roasting pan out of the oven and set it on a heat-proof surface. Using a pot holder, tilt the pan slightly so the fat runs to one corner. Use a meat baster to take up the fat. Then empty the fat into a glass measuring cup or metal can.

3 To carve the duck Oriental style, use a very sharp cleaver to cut the roasted duck in half lengthwise through the breast. Use kitchen shears to finish cutting, if necessary. Cut off the wings and legs close to the body.

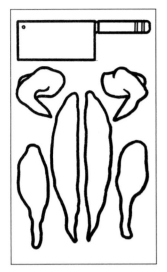

4 Cut the backbone off each half of the bird. Cut each part of the backbone into small pieces by cutting through both meat and bone. Reassemble on an ovenproof serving platter. Next cut each reserved wing and leg into 2 or 3 pieces. Arrange in original shape on platter, as shown.

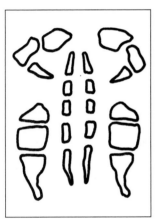

5 Cut the remaining duck halves in half lengthwise. Then cut each of these strips into small pieces, as shown. Reassemble each half into its original shape on the platter, as shown on pages 102-103.

Cherry Roasted Goose

You'll find apple-cherry juice in the baby food aisle of the grocery store.

1 **8- to 10-pound domestic goose**
2 **tablespoons lemon juice**
¾ **cup apple-cherry juice**
⅓ **cup sugar**
9 **inches stick cinnamon**
6 **whole cloves**
1 **tablespoon cornstarch**
1 **16-ounce package frozen unsweetened pitted tart red cherries, thawed and drained,** *or* **one 16-ounce can pitted tart red cherries (water pack), drained**
2 **tablespoons brandy** *or* **Kirsch**

Rinse goose; pat dry. Season cavity with salt. Tuck drumsticks under the band of skin across the tail. Skewer neck skin to back. Twist wing tips under back. Prick skin well (see photo 1).

Place bird, breast side up, on a rack in a roasting pan. Brush with lemon juice. Insert a meat thermometer into the thigh meat (see photo 4, page 17). Roast, uncovered, in a 350° oven for 2¾ to 3¼ hours or till meat thermometer registers 180° to 185° (see photo 4, page 9). Remove fat during roasting (see photo 2). Cover; let stand for 15 minutes before carving (see page 19).

Meanwhile, for sauce, combine apple-cherry juice, sugar, cinnamon, and cloves. Bring to boiling. Reduce heat; cover and simmer 15 minutes. Remove spices. Combine cornstarch and 1 tablespoon *cold water;* add to juice mixture. Cook and stir till thickened and bubbly, then cook and stir 2 minutes more. Add cherries and brandy; heat through. Pass sauce. Serves 10.

Cherry Roasted Duck: Prepare Cherry Roasted Goose as above, *except* substitute one 4- to 5-pound *domestic duckling* for goose and halve remaining ingredients, using ⅓ *cup* apple-cherry juice. Roast, uncovered, in a 375° oven for 1¾ to 2¼ hours or till meat thermometer registers 180° to 185° (see photo 4, page 9). Makes 6 servings.

Roasted Split Chicken

If you're planning a party and looking for something showy to serve your company, look no further.

We've found an innovative technique that's sure to impress—placing stuffing between the skin and flesh of a bird. There's a lot of room under the skin, and we've filled it with some of the tastiest stuffings around.

Serve one of these birds to your next dinner guests. They'll agree it's a real knockout!

Swiss Cheese- and
Ham-Stuffed Split Chicken

Swiss Cheese-
And Ham-Stuffed
Split Chicken

1 **beaten egg**
¾ **cup soft bread crumbs (1 slice)**
½ **cup diced fully cooked ham**
½ **cup shredded Swiss cheese (2 ounces)**
1 **4-ounce can chopped mushrooms,**
   drained
2 **tablespoons milk**
1 **2½- to 3-pound broiler-fryer chicken**
   Cooking oil *or* melted butter
   Tomato roses (optional)
   Watercress (optional)

For stuffing, in a bowl combine egg, bread crumbs, ham, cheese, mushrooms, and milk.

Rinse bird, then pat dry. With poultry shears, cut closely along 1 side of backbone. Repeat on other side (see photo 1). Discard backbone.

Turn bird breast side up; open out so drumstick tips point out. Cover breast with clear plastic wrap. Pound firmly in center (see photo 2). At neck and on 1 side of breast, slip fingers under skin to loosen it from meat; work toward tail (see photo 3). Repeat on other side of breast.

At neck, push stuffing under skin. Stuff drumstick-thigh area, then breast. Shape into place from outside. Secure neck skin to back.

Make 2 slits in the skin on each side of the bird, 1 inch from the edge of the bird, near tail end. Push drumstick ends through the slits (see photo 4). Twist wing tips under. Smooth stuffing to follow the curve of the bird.

Place bird, breast side up, on a rack in a shallow roasting pan. Brush with oil or butter. Insert a meat thermometer (see photo 4, page 17). Roast, uncovered, in a 375° oven 1 to 1¼ hours or till thermometer registers 180° to 185° (see photo 4, page 9). Cover; let stand 15 minutes.

To carve, cut gently through skin and stuffing down center of breast. Split each half by slicing between thighs and breast. If desired, garnish with tomato roses and watercress. Serves 4.

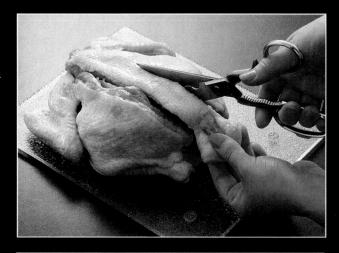

1 Use poultry shears to cut closely along one side of the backbone along the entire length of bird. Repeat on other side, as shown.

Or, with bird breast side up, insert a long knife into the body cavity close to one side of backbone. Press down hard with a rocking motion to cut through. Repeat on other side.

2 With the breast side up, open the bird out as much as possible. Cover with clear plastic wrap. Strike breast firmly in the center with the flat side of a meat mallet. This breaks the bones so bird lies flat.

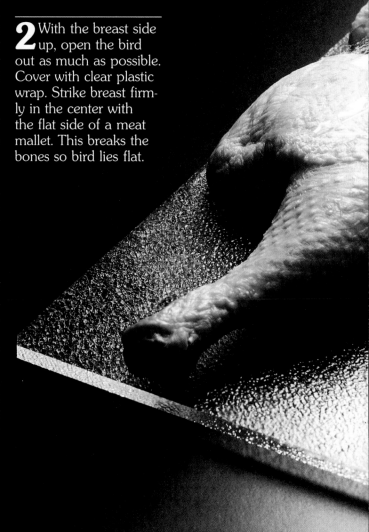

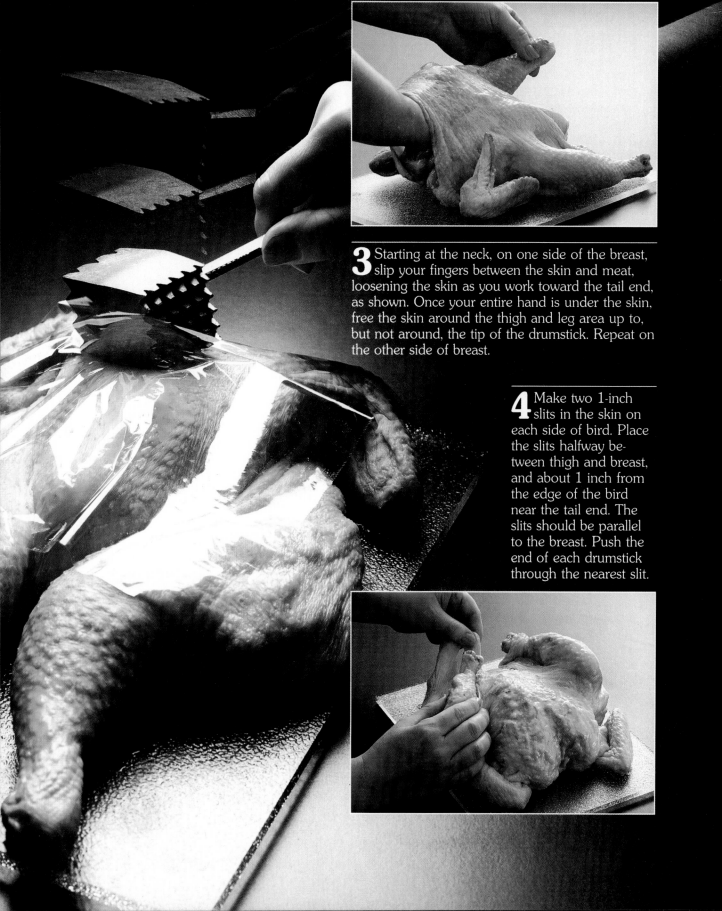

3 Starting at the neck, on one side of the breast, slip your fingers between the skin and meat, loosening the skin as you work toward the tail end, as shown. Once your entire hand is under the skin, free the skin around the thigh and leg area up to, but not around, the tip of the drumstick. Repeat on the other side of breast.

4 Make two 1-inch slits in the skin on each side of bird. Place the slits halfway between thigh and breast, and about 1 inch from the edge of the bird near the tail end. The slits should be parallel to the breast. Push the end of each drumstick through the nearest slit.

Four-Cheese-Stuffed Split Chicken

⅔ cup ricotta cheese
½ cup shredded mozzarella cheese
½ cup shredded provolone cheese
¼ cup grated Romano *or* Parmesan cheese
¼ cup snipped parsley
2 tablespoons fine dry bread crumbs
1 2½- to 3-pound broiler-fryer chicken
Cooking oil *or* melted butter

For stuffing, in a medium bowl combine ricotta, mozzarella, provolone, and Romano or Parmesan cheeses with parsley and bread crumbs.

Rinse bird, then pat dry. With poultry shears, cut closely along 1 side of backbone. Repeat (*see* photo 1, page 108). Discard backbone.

Turn bird breast side up; open out so drumstick tips point out. Cover breast with clear plastic wrap. Pound firmly in center (*see* photo 2, page 108). At neck and on 1 side of breast, slip fingers under skin to loosen it from meat; work toward the tail (*see* photo 3, page 109). Repeat on other side of breast.

At neck, push stuffing under skin. Stuff drumstick-thigh area, then breast. Shape into place from outside. Secure neck skin to back.

Make 2 slits in the skin on each side of the bird, 1 inch from the edge of the bird, near tail end. Push drumstick ends through the slits (*see* photo 4, page 109). Twist wing tips under. With hands, smooth and shape stuffing to follow the curve of the bird.

Place bird, breast side up, on a rack in a shallow roasting pan. Brush with oil or butter. Insert a meat thermometer (*see* photo 4, page 17). Roast, uncovered, in a 375° oven 1 to 1¼ hours or till thermometer registers 180° to 185° (*see* photo 4, page 9). Cover; let stand 15 minutes.

To carve, cut gently through skin and stuffing down center of breast. Split each half by slicing between thighs and breast. Makes 4 servings.

Stuffed Split Chicken

Spinach and Bacon Stuffing, Sausage-Wheat Stuffing, *or* Tandoori Stuffing (see page 111)
1 **2½- to 3-pound broiler-fryer chicken Cooking oil *or* melted butter**

Prepare Spinach and Bacon Stuffing, Sausage-Wheat Stuffing, or Tandoori Stuffing. Set aside.

Rinse bird, then pat dry. With poultry shears, cut closely along 1 side of backbone. Repeat (*see* photo 1, page 108). Discard backbone.

Turn bird breast side up; open out so drumstick tips point out. Cover breast with clear plastic wrap. Pound firmly in center (*see* photo 2, page 108). At neck and on 1 side of breast, slip fingers under skin to loosen it from meat; work toward the tail (*see* photo 3, page 109). Repeat on other side of breast.

At neck, push stuffing under skin. Stuff drumstick-thigh area, then breast. Shape into place from outside. Secure neck skin to back.

Make 2 slits in the skin on each side of the bird, 1 inch from the edge of the bird, near tail end. Push drumstick ends through the slits (*see* photo 4, page 109). Twist wing tips under. With hands, smooth and shape stuffing to follow the curve of the bird.

Place bird, breast side up, on a rack in a shallow roasting pan. Brush with oil or butter. Insert a meat thermometer (*see* photo 4, page 17). Roast, uncovered, in a 375° oven 1 to 1¼ hours or till thermometer registers 180° to 185° (*see* photo 4, page 9). Cover; let stand 15 minutes.

To carve, cut gently through skin and stuffing down center of breast. Split each half by slicing between thighs and breast. Makes 4 servings.

Spinach and Bacon Stuffing

A colorful stuffing that mimics the flavors of a wilted spinach salad.

1 **10-ounce package frozen chopped spinach, thawed and well drained**
4 **slices bacon, crisp-cooked, drained, and crumbled**
½ **cup finely shredded carrot**
½ **cup sliced green onion**
⅓ **cup soft bread crumbs**
¼ **cup toasted chopped almonds**
1 **beaten egg**
2 **tablespoons butter *or* margarine, melted**
⅛ **teaspoon salt**
⅛ **teaspoon pepper**

In a medium bowl combine spinach, bacon, carrot, green onion, bread crumbs, almonds, egg, butter or margarine, salt, and pepper. Use to stuff one 2½- to 3-pound broiler-fryer chicken, as directed in Stuffed Split Chicken (see recipe, page 110).

Sausage-Wheat Stuffing

Sunflower nuts add crunch to the whole-grain stuffing.

¾ **cup beef broth**
⅓ **cup finely shredded carrot**
1 **small onion, chopped (⅓ cup)**
⅓ **cup bulgur wheat**
½ **cup chopped summer sausage (3 ounces)**
2 **tablespoons sunflower nuts**
½ **teaspoon poultry seasoning**
  Dash pepper

In a small saucepan combine broth, carrot, and onion. Bring to boiling. Reduce heat, then cover and simmer about 3 minutes or till vegetables are tender.

Remove from heat. Stir in bulgur. Cover, then let stand 15 minutes. Stir in sausage, sunflower nuts, poultry seasoning, and pepper. Use to stuff one 2½- to 3-pound broiler-fryer chicken, as directed in Stuffed Split Chicken (see recipe, page 110).

Tandoori Stuffing

This flavor-packed stuffing may seem dry when you mix it, but it will become moist during cooking.

1 **medium onion, finely chopped (½ cup)**
2 **cloves garlic, minced**
2 **tablespoons butter *or* margarine**
¼ **cup plain yogurt**
1 **teaspoon ground coriander**
½ **teaspoon finely shredded lemon peel**
½ **teaspoon ground cumin**
½ **teaspoon ground ginger**
¼ **teaspoon salt**
¼ **teaspoon turmeric**
⅛ **teaspoon ground red pepper**
½ **cup fine dry bread crumbs**

In a small saucepan cook onion and garlic in hot butter or margarine till tender but not brown; cool.

In a small bowl stir together yogurt, coriander, lemon peel, cumin, ginger, salt, turmeric, and red pepper. Add onion mixture and bread crumbs, then mix well. Use to stuff one 2½- to 3-pound broiler-fryer chicken, as directed in Stuffed Split Chicken (see recipe, page 110).

Stuffed Boneless Chicken

Imagine a gloriously golden roasted bird on a platter in the center of your table. It's a beautiful sight. And we've made this spectacular entrée extra special by boning the entire bird first.

Then, to retain the bird's shape, we've filled it to the brim with a luscious, moist stuffing. Of course, an elegant boneless chicken is only one benefit you receive from this artful boning technique. A bird minus the bones carves easily and is easier to eat.

Boned Chicken Élégant

Boned Chicken
Élégant

1 2½- to 3-pound broiler-fryer chicken
1 medium onion, chopped (½ cup)
¼ cup butter *or* margarine
1 teaspoon poultry seasoning
4 cups dry raisin bread cubes (6 slices)
½ cup unsweetened pineapple juice
**1 6-ounce package (1½ cups) mixed dried
    fruit bits**
**3 tablespoons snipped parsley
    Cooking oil *or* melted butter**

Set bird on tail. At *inside* of neck opening, find joints attaching wings to back. Make cuts to expose bones; cut through joints (see photo 1). At same place, cut through joint connecting breastbone and back. Leave wings intact.

Loosen meat from wishbone; remove wishbone (see photo 2). Work finger along breastbone to free meat from bone (see photo 3).

Work fingers around rib cage to back and as far down backbone as you can, loosening meat and cutting cartilage as needed (see photo 4). Break ribs; remove (see photo 5).

Loosen or cut remaining meat from backbone. On the inside of the bird cut across bottom of the backbone to separate the tail and the backbone, leaving the tail attached, if desired. Break joints connecting lower backbone to thighbones. Cut through joints (see photo 6). Remove remaining backbone and attached rib cage (see photo 7).

Break leg-thigh joints. Loosen meat from thighbones; remove thighbones (see photo 8). If any meat comes out with bones, remove it from bones; return it to cavity. Rinse bird; pat dry.

In a small saucepan cook onion in hot butter or margarine till tender but not brown. Remove from heat; stir in poultry seasoning, ¼ teaspoon *salt*, and dash *pepper*. In a large mixing bowl combine onion mixture and bread cubes. Drizzle with juice. Add fruit and parsley. Set aside.

Lay bird breast side down. With needle and thread, sew back skin closed if it has been torn. Sew neck closed; secure thread. Spoon fruit mixture into cavity. Carefully turn bird breast side up. Sew bottom opening closed.

Tie legs to tail. Twist wing tips under. Insert skewer through wings and breast. Insert skewer through thighs and body cavity. With twine, tie skewers in figure-8 pattern on back of bird. Insert meat thermometer into the meat in the thigh area (see photo 4, page 17).

Place bird, breast side up, on a rack in a shallow roasting pan. Brush with oil or melted butter. Roast, uncovered, in a 375° oven 1¼ to 1¾ hours or till meat thermometer registers 180° to 185° (see photo 4, page 9). Remove skewers, twine, and thread. Cover; let stand 15 minutes. To carve, cut bird into quarters. Garnish with red grapes, if desired. Makes 4 servings.

Boned Turkey Élégant: Prepare Boned Chicken Élégant as above, *except* substitute one 8- to 9-pound *turkey* for chicken; double remaining ingredients. Roast, uncovered, in a 325° oven 2 to 3 hours or till meat thermometer registers 180° to 185° in the thigh (see photo 4, page 9). To carve, remove drumsticks and wings. Slice thigh meat. Cut turkey in half lengthwise down center of breast. Cut crosswise into 1-inch slices. Makes 16 servings.

1 Starting from the inside of the neck opening, use your fingers to find the joints where the wings attach to the back. With a small sharp knife, make a cut just *inside* the neck opening on each side of the bird to expose the bones that form these joints. Cut through the joints and ligaments, as shown.

2 Loosen the meat from the wishbone with your fingers. Use a knife or kitchen shears to cut the ligaments as necessary. Remove the wishbone. It may be necessary to cut the wishbone away from the breastbone.

3 Work your index finger down along each side of the breastbone, freeing the meat from the bone as you go. Use a knife to loosen the white cartilage from the skin, if necessary, to release the breastbone.

4 Work your fingers around the rib cage to the back and as far down the backbone as you can. Loosen the meat and cut the cartilage, if necessary. Turn the bird over to make detaching the meat from the backbone easier.

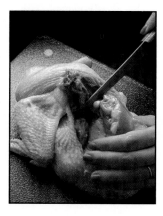

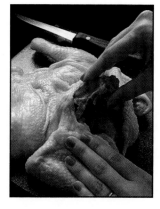

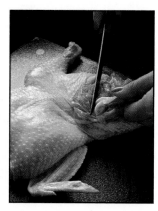

5 With your fingers, break the portion of the ribs and backbone that have been freed of meat. Remove them through the opening, along with the attached breastbone, as shown.

6 Break the joints that connect the lower backbone to the thighbones. Pull the meat away from the joints and cut through the ligaments at the joints.

7 Remove the remaining portion of the rib cage and backbone. For larger birds, such as turkeys, it is easiest to remove the rib cage-backbone portions through the larger bottom opening of the bird.

8 Break the joints between the legs and thighs. From the inside of the bird, loosen or scrape the meat from the thighbones, cutting the ligaments as necessary. Remove the thighbones, as shown.

Mix 'n' Match Stuffings

You've heard of custom cars and custom furniture. Now you can have a custom roasted bird.

Simply choose whatever size and type of bird you'd like to prepare. Then fill it with one of these delicious stuffings and roast according to the directions given on pages 118 and 119.

Let's say you're having 10 guests for dinner. You may choose to prepare a 5- to 6-pound capon and stuff it with a single recipe of Chestnut Stuffing. But if you're planning a more intimate gathering of four friends, simply halve the recipe and use it for two 1- to 1½-pound Cornish game hens.

Cranberry-Apple Stuffing

If you don't have store-bought apple pie spice, use our homemade version given below.

5	cups dry whole wheat bread cubes (about 7 slices)
4	medium apples, peeled, cored, and chopped (3½ cups)
½	cup chopped pitted dates
½	teaspoon apple pie spice *or* Homemade Apple Pie Spice*
⅔	cup apple juice
½	cup cranberry-orange relish

In a large mixing bowl combine bread cubes, apples, dates, and apple pie spice. Stir juice into cranberry-orange relish. Drizzle over bread-fruit mixture, then toss lightly till well mixed. Stuff one 8- to 10-pound domestic goose, *or* two 4- to 5-pound domestic ducklings.

Measure any remaining stuffing. For *each* cup, stir in an extra *1 tablespoon* apple juice. Place in a casserole. Cover and chill. Bake, covered, the last 20 to 40 minutes of birds' roasting time. Makes 8 cups stuffing.

*Homemade Apple Pie Spice:** Combine ¼ teaspoon ground *cinnamon,* ⅛ teaspoon ground *nutmeg,* dash ground *cloves,* and dash ground *allspice or* ground *ginger* and use in place of the ½ teaspoon apple pie spice.

Chestnut Stuffing

The baking time for the casserole of leftover stuffing will vary with the amount of stuffing in it. A cup of stuffing will take only 20 minutes, and several cups may take the full 40 minutes.

**4 ounces fresh chestnuts *or* ½ of a
        4-ounce package dried chestnuts**
½ cup chopped celery
1 small onion, chopped (⅓ cup)
¼ cup butter *or* margarine
½ teaspoon ground sage
⅛ teaspoon pepper
**½ of a 16-ounce loaf French *or*
        Italian bread, cut into ½-inch cubes
        and toasted**
¾ cup chicken broth
2 tablespoons water*
2 tablespoons dry vermouth *or* dry sherry*

If using fresh chestnuts, cut an X in the flat side of each chestnut. Place in a medium saucepan; cover with cold water. Bring to boiling. Reduce heat, then cover and simmer for 10 to 15 minutes. Drain. When cool enough to handle, peel and chop. If using dried chestnuts, cook according to package directions and chop.

Meanwhile, in a small saucepan cook celery and onion in hot butter or margarine till tender but not brown. Stir in sage and pepper. In a large mixing bowl combine chestnuts and bread cubes; stir in vegetable mixture. Drizzle with broth, water, and vermouth or sherry, then toss lightly till well mixed.

Stuff one 5- to 6-pound roasting chicken *or* one 5- to 6-pound capon. *Or,* halve all ingredients, using *3 tablespoons* onion and *⅓ cup* broth, and stuff one 2½- to 3-pound broiler-fryer chicken *or* two 2- to 3-pound pheasant *or* two 1- to 1½-pound Cornish game hens *or* eight 4- to 6-ounce quail. *Or,* double all ingredients and stuff one 10- to 12-pound turkey.

Measure any remaining stuffing. For *each* cup, stir in an extra *2 teaspoons* chicken broth. Place in a casserole. Cover and chill. Bake, covered, the last 20 to 40 minutes of birds' roasting time. Single recipe makes about 6 cups stuffing.

***Note:** If desired, omit water and vermouth; use an additional ¼ cup chicken broth.

Poultry Roasting Chart

Poultry	Ready-to-Cook Weight	Oven Temp.	Guide to Roasting Time	Special Instructions
Chicken	2½-3 lbs. 3½-4 lbs. 4½-5 lbs.	375° 375° 375°	1¼-1½ hrs. 1¾-2 hrs. 2¼-2½ hrs.	Brush dry areas of skin occasionally with pan drippings.
Roasting Chicken	5-6 lbs.	325°	2½-3 hrs.	Cover *loosely* with foil. Uncover last half of roasting. Brush as above.
Capon	5-7 lbs.	325°	1¾-2½ hrs.	Roast as for roasting chicken.
Cornish Game Hen	1-1½ lbs.	375°	1¼-1½ hrs.	Cover *loosely* with foil; roast for ½ hour. Uncover; roast 45 to 55 minutes more or till done. If desired, baste occasionally the last hour.
Stuffed Turkey*	6-8 lbs. 8-12 lbs. 12-16 lbs. 16-20 lbs. 20-24 lbs.	325° 325° 325° 325° 325°	3-3½ hrs. 3½-4½ hrs. 4-5 hrs. 4½-5½ hrs. 5-6½ hrs.	Cover bird *loosely* with foil. Press lightly at the end of drumsticks and neck; leave an air space between bird and foil. Baste bird occasionally, if desired. Uncover the last 45 minutes of roasting.
Domestic Duckling	3-5 lbs.	375°	1½-2¼ hrs.	Roast as for domestic goose.
Domestic Goose	7-8 lbs. 8-10 lbs. 10-12 lbs.	350° 350° 350°	2½-2¾ hrs. 2¾-3¼ hrs. 3¼-4 hrs.	Prick skin well all over. During roasting, spoon off excess fat. *Do not rub with oil.*
Quail	4-6 oz.	375°	40-50 min.	Split quail down backbone and open slightly for ease in stuffing. Cover *loosely* with foil entire time.
Pheasant	2-3 lb.	350°	1½-1¾ hrs.	Lay slices of bacon over breast. Remove bacon and baste frequently the last 15 minutes.
Squab	12-14 oz.	375°	1-1¼ hrs.	Cover *loosely* with foil and roast for ½ hour. Uncover and roast 30 to 40 minutes more or till done.

Birds vary in size, shape, and tenderness. Use these times as a general guide to roasting your bird.
*Unstuffed turkeys generally require 30 to 45 minutes less total roasting time than stuffed turkeys.

Roasting Instructions

Preparation for roasting:
Rinse the bird; pat dry with paper towels (see photo 1, page 9). Rub cavities with *salt,* if desired. Do not stuff until just before cooking.

To stuff the bird, spoon some stuffing loosely into neck cavity (see photo 1, page 16). Pull the neck skin to the back of the bird; fasten securely with a small skewer (see photo 2, page 16). Lightly spoon the remaining stuffing into the body cavity. If the opening has a band of skin across the tail, tuck the drumsticks under the band (see photo 3, page 17). *Or,* tie legs securely to tail. Twist the wing tips under the back (see photo 3, page 9).

For an unstuffed bird, place quartered vegetables in the body cavity, if you like. Tie legs together; pull neck skin to back and twist wing tips under (see photo 3, page 9). Roast. Discard vegetables.

Roasting directions:
Place the bird, breast side up, on a rack in a shallow roasting pan. Brush the skin of the bird, *except* domestic duckling or goose, with cooking oil or melted butter. Prick the skin of a duckling or goose well all over to allow fat to escape during roasting (see photo 1, page 104). If using a meat thermometer, insert it in the center of the inside thigh muscle, making sure the bulb does not touch the bone (see photo 4, page 17).

Roast, uncovered (unless specified otherwise), according to the chart opposite. When the bird is two-thirds done, cut the band of skin or string between the legs so the thighs will cook evenly. Continue roasting until the bird is done (see photo 4, page 9). Remove the bird from the oven; cover loosely with foil to keep warm. Let stand 15 to 20 minutes before carving (see page 19).

Test for doneness:
See photo 4 on page 9 for a description of doneness tests.

To roast turkey in a covered roasting pan:
Rinse the turkey; pat dry (see photo 1, page 9). Stuff, if you like (see photos 1–3, pages 16–17). Prepare for roasting as directed at left and in the chart opposite. Place the turkey, breast side up, on a rack in a roasting pan. Brush with cooking oil or melted butter. Insert a meat thermometer in the center of the inside thigh muscle (see photo 4, page 17). Do not add water. Cover the pan *tightly* with foil or with a lid. Roast the bird in a 350° oven till about three-fourths done. Remove the cover; cut the band of skin or string between the legs. Baste the turkey with the pan drippings. Continue roasting, uncovered, till done (see photo 4, page 9). The turkey will not be as golden as when roasted loosely covered.

To roast turkey in a commercial cooking bag:
Rinse the turkey; pat dry (see photo 1, page 9). Stuff, if you like (see photos 1–3, pages 16–17). Prepare for roasting as directed at left and in the chart opposite. Put 1 tablespoon all-purpose flour in the commercial cooking bag, then shake to coat the inside. Place the bag in a large roasting pan. Brush the turkey with cooking oil or melted butter. Place the turkey inside the bag, breast side up. Close the bag loosely with a twist tie. Make six ½-inch slits in the top of the bag to allow steam to escape. Roast according to the manufacturer's directions. About 15 minutes before the end of roasting time, cut the bag open. Insert a meat thermometer in the center of the inside thigh muscle (see photo 4, page 17). Continue roasting till done (see photo 4, page 9).

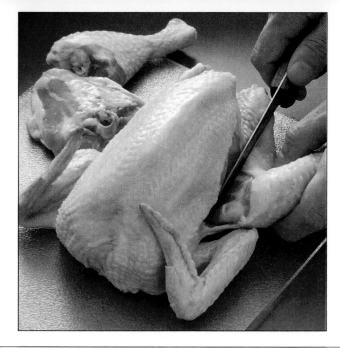

Cutting Up A Whole Chicken

Cutting up a whole chicken is one of those cooking techniques that can be a total mystery. The truth is, it's really not mysterious or hard to do.

To prove it, we've provided clear-cut instructions along with accompanying step-by-step photographs. Simply sharpen your knife and follow along.

By cutting up your own chicken, you may save up to 20 cents on every pound of bird you buy. And you'll get the type and number of pieces you want—all great rewards for a few swift fells of the knife!

1 Hold the tip of a drumstick and pull the leg away from the body. As you are doing this, use a sharp knife to cut through the skin between the thigh and body. Next, hold the body firmly with one hand. Use the other hand to bend the thigh back until the thighbone pops out of the hip joint. Then cut through the broken joint in order to separate the leg from the body, as shown. Cut as close to the backbone as possible. To separate the thigh from the drumstick, slit the skin above the knee joint. Break this joint by bending the leg and thigh together. Cut through the broken joint. Repeat on the other side.

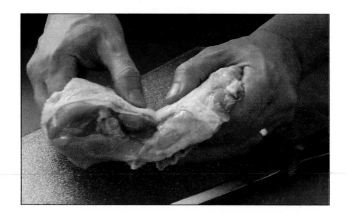

4 To divide the back in half, hold the piece at each end. Bend the ends toward the skin side of the back until the bones break, as shown. Cut the back in half where the bones are broken. If you like, cut off the tail.

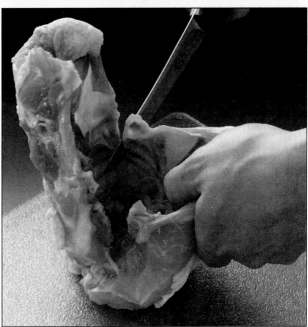

2 Use one hand to pull a wing away from the body. At the same time, slit the skin between the wing and body. Next, bend the wing back until the wing-body joint breaks. Cut through the broken joint, as shown. Repeat on the other side.

3 Now separate the breast from the back. Use a sharp knife or kitchen shears to cut along the breast end of the ribs on one side. Cut from the lower end of the chicken toward the neck end as far as you can, as shown. Repeat on the other side. Bend the front and back halves apart, exposing the joints at the neck which connect the two halves. Cut through the joints.

5 Divide the breast in half by cutting lengthwise along the breastbone. *Or,* to divide the breast in half crosswise, grasp the breast at each end as for the back. Bend the ends toward the skin side until the bones break. Cut the breast in half crosswise between the wishbone and breastbone, as shown.

Nutrition Analysis Chart

Use these analyses to compare nutritional values of different recipes. This information was calculated using Agriculture Handbook Number 456, published by the United States Department of Agriculture, as the primary source.

In compiling the nutrition analyses, we made the following assumptions:
- For all of the main-dish meat recipes, the nutrition analyses were calculated using weights or measures for cooked meat.

- Garnishes and optional ingredients were not included in the nutrition analyses.
- If a marinade was brushed over a food during cooking, the analysis includes all of the marinade.
- When two ingredient options appear in a recipe, calculations were made using the first one.
- For ingredients of variable weight (such as "2½- to 3-pound broiler-fryer chicken") or for recipes with a serving range ("makes 4 to 6 servings"), calculations were made using the first figure.

	Per Serving						Percent USRDA Per Serving							
	Calories	Protein (g)	Carbohydrate (g)	Fat (g)	Sodium (mg)	Potassium (mg)	Protein	Vitamin A	Vitamin C	Thiamine	Riboflavin	Niacin	Calcium	Iron
Chicken														
Apple Broiled Chicken (p. 48)	194	24	9	6	29	10	37	19	1	6	29	36	2	15
Barbecue-Style Broiled Drumsticks (p. 48)	240	33	6	9	199	76	50	34	4	9	40	50	3	20
Barbecued Pineapple Bake (p. 68)	259	25	11	12	349	96	39	21	24	10	31	38	3	16
Barbecued Pineapple Chicken Bake (p. 68)	259	25	11	12	349	96	39	21	24	10	31	38	3	16
Beer Batter-Fried Chicken (p. 94)	372	32	22	16	610	399	50	18	0	14	39	49	3	18
Boned Chicken Élégant (p. 114)	618	41	58	26	438	581	63	105	22	20	54	66	10	41
Broiled Chicken-Vegetable Kabobs (p. 54)	236	23	25	6	417	530	35	83	31	10	17	44	5	12
Cabbage-Apple Chicken Burritos (p. 79)	387	27	29	18	236	186	42	17	31	8	22	42	24	15
Cantaloupe Chicken Salad (p. 28)	398	27	24	23	433	1121	41	186	153	12	15	51	9	15
Cheesy Caraway Chicken (p. 34)	306	32	20	10	335	46	49	5	0	13	20	59	13	13
Cheesy Macaroni Casserole (p. 63)	369	23	21	21	517	380	36	102	9	18	24	24	30	12
Chicken and Brown Rice in Tomatoes (p. 30)	524	25	30	35	889	807	39	41	77	15	13	42	6	16
Chicken and Noodles (p. 100)	272	29	20	8	645	139	44	35	41	18	40	43	6	20
Chicken and Vegetable Platter (p. 76)	332	32	12	18	282	325	49	30	65	16	27	64	6	28
Chicken Cacciatore (p. 68)	407	31	39	12	239	463	47	46	39	34	43	55	5	28
Chicken Cordon Bleu (p. 86)	553	32	28	34	752	278	50	22	2	29	33	45	34	16
Chicken Divan-Style (p. 61)	267	25	8	15	391	377	38	36	57	7	21	22	35	8
Chicken in Herbed Tomato Sauce (p. 24)	175	23	7	6	443	102	35	32	17	8	28	37	2	15
Chicken in Red Wine Sauce (p. 69)	242	25	6	9	22	144	38	72	7	8	30	37	3	16
Chicken Kiev (p. 89)	299	23	12	17	524	302	35	13	0	8	13	48	3	10
Chicken Macaroni Salad (p. 30)	492	33	30	27	425	656	51	62	72	23	21	50	8	18
Chicken Primavera (p. 60)	510	33	57	17	517	768	50	99	135	45	41	45	33	21
Chicken Salad Croissants (p. 31)	416	22	35	21	632	313	34	13	20	19	16	30	5	17

	Per Serving						Percent USRDA Per Serving							
	Calories	Protein (g)	Carbohydrate (g)	Fat (g)	Sodium (mg)	Potassium (mg)	Protein	Vitamin A	Vitamin C	Thiamine	Riboflavin	Niacin	Calcium	Iron

Chicken *(continued)*

	Calories	Protein (g)	Carbohydrate (g)	Fat (g)	Sodium (mg)	Potassium (mg)	Protein	Vitamin A	Vitamin C	Thiamine	Riboflavin	Niacin	Calcium	Iron
Chicken Soup Élégant (p. 61)	350	23	17	19	560	490	36	15	8	8	21	30	17	7
Chicken Soup with Matzo Balls (p. 101)	301	28	16	13	634	321	43	64	17	12	36	38	7	21
Chicken Tempura with Ginger Tempura Sauce (p. 94)	320	31	31	8	911	732	48	30	104	21	34	60	10	19
Chicken-Vegetable Kabobs (p. 54)	236	23	25	6	417	530	35	83	31	10	17	44	5	12
Chicken with Marsala (p. 83)	244	29	7	9	122	42	45	11	7	8	15	56	2	11
Cordon Bleu Casserole (p. 62)	466	31	28	25	555	448	48	25	13	27	36	31	43	15
Covered Fried Chicken (p. 43)	218	25	4	11	1	5	38	19	0	8	30	37	2	16
Crab-Stuffed Chicken Rolls (p. 89)	268	29	6	13	218	234	44	36	19	12	18	44	9	11
Creamed Chicken Stew with Cornmeal Dumplings (p. 101)	431	31	29	21	510	202	48	32	19	24	42	45	13	23
Crisp Chip Chicken (p. 36)	230	26	7	10	37	100	40	21	2	8	32	38	4	16
Crispy Chicken Fiesta Platter (p. 40)	226	25	5	11	190	73	38	34	9	9	31	38	3	16
Crusty Cornmeal Chicken Thighs (p. 43)	197	18	9	9	178	46	28	14	4	10	23	27	2	12
Curry-and Wine-Sauced Chicken (p. 25)	179	28	2	3	2	35	44	2	0	5	16	56	2	11
Deep-Fried Cornmeal Chicken (p. 95)	401	34	23	18	594	445	52	19	0	13	40	48	8	16
Dill-Buttered Chicken (p. 12)	193	24	0	10	47	1	37	22	0	6	29	36	2	14
Down-Home Fried Chicken (p. 43)	218	25	4	11	1	5	38	19	0	8	30	37	2	15
Easy Chicken Fiesta Platter (p. 40)	226	25	5	11	190	73	38	34	9	9	31	38	3	16
Easy Curry-Apple Chicken (p. 69)	505	33	60	16	385	124	50	27	6	17	37	54	7	34
Four-Cheese-Stuffed Chicken (p. 110)	439	51	6	23	264	116	78	42	10	10	57	55	41	24
Four-Spice Chicken (p. 10)	199	24	0	11	0	0	37	19	0	6	29	36	2	14
Fried Chicken Fiesta Platter (p. 40)	226	25	5	11	190	73	38	34	9	9	31	38	3	16
Garlic Roasted Chicken (p. 10)	179	24	0	9	21	0	37	19	0	6	29	36	2	14
Grilled Orange-Ginger Chicken (p. 46)	255	28	29	3	405	38	44	3	6	5	14	53	3	12
Hawaiian-Style Fried Chicken (p. 42)	508	34	52	19	638	250	52	7	33	27	19	63	5	22
Herbed Batter-Fried Chicken (p. 92)	398	33	16	22	346	427	51	18	0	12	40	48	8	16
Herbed Fried Chicken (p. 42)	233	25	6	11	240	25	39	22	5	8	31	38	3	16
Hickory Barbecued Halves (p. 52)	198	24	6	8	292	8	37	24	2	6	29	37	2	14
Home-Style Chicken and Dumplings (p. 98)	348	29	28	13	546	197	45	47	14	21	40	45	12	22
Indian-Style Oven-Fried Chicken (p. 37)	314	28	10	19	136	121	43	23	0	10	30	47	3	17
Lemon-Dill Chicken Breasts (p. 78)	174	28	0	6	67	6	43	4	3	5	13	54	2	9
Lemon-Tarragon Fricassee (p. 72)	285	26	5	17	221	159	40	32	17	8	33	37	6	18
Maple-Orange Barbecued Chicken (p. 55)	218	24	14	7	191	79	38	20	18	8	30	36	4	16
Maple-Orange Broiled Chicken (p. 55)	218	24	14	7	191	79	38	20	18	8	30	36	4	16
Mushroom-Wine-Sauced Breasts (p. 78)	256	30	4	12	256	130	46	8	1	7	20	58	3	12
Orange-Ginger Glazed Chicken (p. 46)	255	28	29	3	405	38	44	3	6	5	14	53	3	12
Orange Oriental Chicken (p. 79)	388	33	39	11	1430	235	51	9	42	23	19	64	5	23
Oven Chicken Cacciatore (p. 68)	407	31	39	12	239	463	47	46	39	34	43	55	5	28
Oven-Fried Potato and Herb Chicken (p. 36)	190	25	7	7	187	128	38	19	4	7	30	38	3	14
Paella-Style Chicken Braise (p. 66)	631	33	42	36	787	349	51	33	76	45	37	52	6	32
Pan-'n'-Oven Fried Chicken (p. 43)	218	25	4	11	1	5	38	19	0	8	30	37	2	15
Peachy Chicken-Filled Pitas (p. 31)	289	26	24	9	159	541	41	38	20	15	16	36	9	15
Roasted Herbed Chicken (p. 8)	180	24	0	9	135	4	37	20	2	6	29	36	2	14
Rum-Raisin-Stuffed Breasts (p. 88)	313	32	20	10	75	254	49	7	2	20	19	57	3	18

	Per Serving					Percent USRDA Per Serving								
	Calories	Protein (g)	Carbohydrate (g)	Fat (g)	Sodium (mg)	Potassium (mg)	Protein	Vitamin A	Vitamin C	Thiamine	Riboflavin	Niacin	Calcium	Iron
Chicken *(continued)*														
Savory-Butter Broiled Chicken (p. 49)	199	28	0	9	102	5	43	7	2	5	13	53	2	9
Sesame Chicken Wings with Sweet-Sour Sauce (p. 95)	63	5	5	3	108	70	8	1	0	2	3	6	1	3
Soy-Sesame Oven-Fried Chicken (p. 37)	208	30	3	8	665	101	46	2	0	6	15	56	3	13
Spanish Rice and Chicken Skillet (p. 62)	453	33	33	21	465	512	51	35	45	14	24	41	31	13
Spicy Cherry-Sauced Chicken (p. 49)	332	24	40	8	98	61	37	21	8	6	30	36	3	17
Spirited Chicken Fricassee (p. 73)	328	27	7	20	277	90	41	29	18	11	36	41	4	17
Stuffed Split Chicken with Sausage-Wheat Stuffing (p. 111)	424	43	15	21	439	177	67	48	4	19	49	63	4	29
Stuffed Split Chicken with Spinach and Bacon Stuffing (p. 111)	451	43	8	27	261	354	66	158	26	17	57	59	13	34
Stuffed Split Chicken with Tandoori Stuffing (p. 111)	386	38	12	19	305	83	59	33	5	12	48	57	6	24
Swiss Cheese- and Ham-Stuffed Split Chicken (p. 108)	425	47	6	23	394	141	72	35	1	18	56	61	18	27
Tortellini & Cream Cheese Sauce (p. 58)	459	30	35	22	550	727	47	36	58	31	41	41	25	16
Turmeric-Poached Chicken (p. 25)	151	28	1	3	317	39	43	9	2	5	13	53	2	10
Wild-Rice-Stuffed Chicken (p. 16)	380	30	25	18	683	133	47	26	6	23	33	45	3	23
Cornish Hens														
Dill-Buttered Cornish Hens (p. 12)	242	29	0	13	70	2	44	27	0	7	34	43	2	16
Honey-Mustard Hens (p. 12)	275	29	9	13	86	9	44	27	0	7	35	43	2	17
Italian Marinated Cornish Hens (p. 54)	278	29	2	14	2	35	44	23	1	7	35	43	2	17
Raisin-Sausage-Stuffed Hens (p. 18)	601	35	27	40	401	325	54	30	23	24	42	50	6	27
Duck and Goose														
Cherry Roasted Duck (p. 105)	246	28	13	8	101	579	43	14	9	7	9	39	2	9
Cherry Roasted Goose (p. 105)	296	33	16	10	121	695	51	17	10	9	11	46	3	11
Roast Duck & Kumquat Sauce (p. 104)	231	28	6	10	182	571	43	9	21	9	9	38	3	9
Pheasant, Quail & Squab														
Bourbon-Sauced Pheasant (p. 18)	514	33	38	23	215	297	51	52	5	19	41	50	6	27
Easy Curry-Apple Pheasant (p. 69)	505	33	60	16	385	124	50	27	6	17	37	54	7	34
Honey-Mustard Squab (p. 12)	234	24	9	11	159	282	37	7	0	4	12	24	1	8
Italian Marinated Pheasant (p. 54)	249	29	1	12	1	23	44	23	0	7	35	43	2	17
Roasted Herbed Quail (p. 8)	216	29	0	10	203	6	44	24	3	7	35	43	2	17
Turkey														
Biscuit-Topped Turkey Pot Pie (p. 60)	337	22	29	15	688	434	34	57	12	15	18	30	9	13
Boned Turkey Élégant (p. 114)	519	36	29	29	327	695	55	48	11	12	21	38	5	22
Cranberry-Sauced Turkey Steaks (p. 24)	283	29	29	4	98	572	45	42	15	5	10	49	4	9
Four-Spice Turkey Breast (p. 10)	204	31	0	8	0	0	48	2	0	5	14	59	2	10
Sweet 'n' Sour Turkey (p. 22)	352	33	37	9	1090	907	50	18	70	17	22	25	10	24
Teriyaki Turkey Thigh (p. 55)	228	30	2	10	1087	449	47	4	0	3	15	21	3	16
Turkey a la King (p. 63)	349	22	23	18	473	409	34	17	26	19	22	29	12	14
Turkey Florentine with Orange Sauce (p. 88)	263	30	16	9	160	545	46	70	32	7	13	50	6	12
Turkey Parmigiana (p. 82)	382	31	21	19	746	485	48	29	27	12	19	41	26	11
Wild-Rice-Stuffed Turkey (p. 16)	595	50	15	36	559	645	77	18	3	18	25	50	3	23
Stuffings														
Chestnut Stuffing (p. 117)	132	3	17	6	246	100	4	4	2	8	5	5	3	5
Cranberry-Apple Stuffing (p. 116)	151	2	36	1	96	185	3	1	7	7	4	5	3	7

Have BETTER HOMES AND
GARDENS® magazine delivered
to your door. For information,
write to: MR. ROBERT AUSTIN
P.O. BOX 4536
DES MOINES, IA 50336